D1743271

Praise for The Coach's Communication Playbook:

"I believe that The Coach's Communication Playbook *is a must in the 90's for coaches at every level."*

-Tim Floyd, Chicago Bulls

"Great idea! The format is easy to use and easy to understand. With the ever-increasing demands on a coach to be an outstanding communicator, this will be a valuable tool."

-Dom Capers, Coach, Carolina Panthers

"This is a brilliant book, authored by someone who has no peer in her profession when it comes to doing what she does best: teaching the art of communication to athletes, coaches, and sports administrators. The Coach's Communication Playbook *will be one of the most popular books ever done in collegiate and high school athletics."*

-Mel Pulliam, Director of Marketing and Development, AFCA

"Kathleen Hessert's strategies and techniques have been an exceptional help to those of us here at the University of Tennessee. I recommend her Coach's Communication Playbook *wholeheartedly."*

-Phillip Fulmer, Head Football Coach, University of Tennessee

"As soon as I looked at the title of The Coach's Communication Playbook, I liked the concept. Once I read it, I was pleased to learn that it is informative, practical and updated for the 90's. I recommend it for anyone who wants to make the job of coaching a little easier."

-Gene Keady, Head Basketball Coach,
Purdue University

"This book is a very realistic and helpful approach for coaches and players working with the media and the public."

-Jerry Green, Basketball Coach,
University of Tennessee

"The Coach's Communication Playbook is simple and easy to follow - with techniques that are easy to apply. It can give a coach the polished edge necessary for those interpersonal relationships that ensure program growth. This is the perfect tool to bring a coach, and their program, to the next level."

-John Simar, Athletic Director,
Charlotte Country Day School

"The Coach's Communication Playbook is a very practical manual that I found to be extremely insightful. It will help you run your team or organization more efficiently and effectively. I've used it myself, and will use it again and again."

-Jim Caldwell, Head Football Coach,
Wake Forest University

"No one addresses how athletes can best communicate to the media and the public better than Kathleen Hessert in The Coach's Communication Playbook. *This essential aid replaces "gut feelings" with a successful action plan."*

-Jim Tunney, Ed.D., Certified Speaking Professional,
former NFL Referee

"For coaches who want to compete and win at the highest level, proper planning and great organization are vital. However, a coach's greatest tool is the ability to communicate effectively in today's society - particularly, with today's athlete. In this regard, Kathleen Hessert's Coach's Communication Playbook *covers every aspect. It's a must read for every coach!"*

-David Odom, Head Basketball Coach,
Wake Forest University

"At a time when all sports, including the non-traditional ones like lacrosse, are receiving more attention, we need both preparation and foresight to keep it all in perspective. The Coach's Communication Playbook *guides you through every facet of communication - and its easy tips are practical enough to fit into a busy coach's schedule."*

-Brad Touma, Varsity Lacrosse Coach,
Charlotte Country Day School

"As coaches, we all know that some days can be so difficult, tying your shoes seems like a challenge. This book can make days like that a little easier. It speaks to coaches at all levels of competition, and provides them with the means to face the new communication challenges they encounter every day.

"One of Kathleen Hessert's abilities is to take complex ideas and simplify them so that anyone can understand and apply them. Hurdles such as the media, the generation gap, and crisis management are easier to jump with the aid of her expertise and experience — and if you're still having trouble with those laces, I'll bet she can help you with that too."

-Charlie Spoonhour, Head Basketball Coach,
St. Louis University

"Communication is a vital ingredient in all aspects of life. The Coach's Communication Playbook is a tremendous tool to help coaches focus and improve on this aspect of their job. It's very practical and helpful in our everyday life — on and off the court. I'm going to use it as required reading for all of our coaches."

-Joan Cronan, Women's Athletic Director,
University of Tennessee

"Who are Kathleen Hessert and Sports Media Challenge?"

Molding communication champions is Kathleen Hessert's business. A former award winning television reporter, talk show host and anchor, Kathleen founded Sports Media Challenge (SMC), a division of Communication Concepts, in 1989. The nationally renowned speaking, training and consulting company based in Charlotte, North Carolina helps sports personalities and organizations maximize success by enhancing media, crisis management, public speaking, and image management skills.

Kathleen is the author of *"Power Training: How to Win at the Media Game"*, *"Winning the Media Game: A Guide for NFL Players"* as well as *"The Pocket Guide to Avoiding Misquotes"*. As a recognized expert for corporations and the sports industry, Kathleen is regularly quoted in national print and broadcast media including USA Today, Sports Business International, TV Guide, ESPN, Athletic Management, Street & Smith's Sports Business, CNN, MSNBC and Fox network.

Kathleen is a regular contributor to American Football Coaches Association publications and has spoken at national conferences including CoSIDA, the Women's Basketball Coaches Association, the Black Coaches Association, National Athletic Directors Association, International Sports Summit, NIKE Championship Basketball Coaches Clinics and many more.

As a speaker, Kathleen is the recipient of the prestigious Certified Speaking Professional designation of the National Speakers Association. Some of her clients include the Universities of Notre Dame, Tennessee & Texas, Olympic legend Dan Jansen, NFL quarterback Peyton Manning, the Charlotte Hornets and NASCAR.

In addition, she is a trustee for the North Carolina Foundation for Health and Physical Fitness and is the founder of the Charlotte Youth Sports Foundation. Kathleen is also a wife and the mother of two student-athletes.

"Why Did I Write This Book?"

I'm not an athletic coach, and I can't and wouldn't tell you how to do your job. However, I am a communication coach. This book marries coaching and communications skills to help you make the most of the opportunities in front of you and develop new ones.

As someone once said, "The biggest room in the world is the room for improvement." No matter how good you already are, to be a winner in the broader sense, you can't just focus on x's and o's anymore. You must develop new skills to provide the edge that sets you and your team apart from the competition. Successful coaches must master skills that enable them to effectively and efficiently address people and situations that were once clearly outside of the coaching responsibility. Modern coaches must master the tools necessary for communicating with a more diverse group of contemporary athletes. Remember that athlete audiences are peopled by the "MTV generation," and they demand concise, dynamic, high impact packaging of ideas. In addition to athletes, you will have to speak to parents, the media, administrators, boosters, fans, and others.

If you're challenged by the demand for new skills and confused about where to find the necessary information, you're not alone. Coaches have asked us for new ways to improve their communication, and now we're offering some answers. In this book, Sports Media Challenge provides forward-thinking coaches with the proven strategies and techniques used by many of today's most dynamic communicators. Because sports is our business, you won't have to struggle with the practical application of these lessons. Everything in this book will apply directly to real world coaching needs.

Sports Media Challenge guarantees that once you try the easy-to-use tips within, you'll be able to express ideas so that others will listen, understand, remember, and take appropriate action. That's an enviable return on anyone's investment.

Kathleen Hessert

Kathleen Hessert
President, Sports Media Challenge

Kathleen Hessert's

COACH'S
Communication
PLAYBOOK

**SPORTS
MEDIA
CHALLENGE**

The Coach's Communication Playbook
First Edition

By Kathleen Hessert With Foreword by Dr. Deborah Yow

Publisher	Sports Media Challenge
Senior Editor	Kathleen Hessert
Project Editor	Cordelia B. Anderson
Cover and Text Design	Leigh Capps

Copyright 1998 by Sports Media Challenge

Address requests for permission to make copies of any part of this book, editorial comments, or orders to: Sports Media Challenge, 2700 Coltsgate Road, Suite 203, Charlotte, North Carolina 28211. 1-800-929-4386

ISBN: 0-964326-52-3

Library of Congress Catalog Card Number: 98-061568

Printed in the United States of America

Dedication

To the hundreds of coaches I've worked with over the years, who shared their passion, concerns and frustrations with me and provided insight into the extraordinary world of coaching.

To Roger Valdiserri, the retired Sports Information Director for the University of Notre Dame, who helped me launch Sports Media Challenge by putting me in front of student-athletes. His initial and ongoing support has meant the world to me.

To my two children Christopher and Meghann, who gave me my first glimpse at the crucial and lasting impact coaches have on athletes' lives.

To my husband and best friend, Tim Gunderman, who shares my dreams and determination and makes everything more fun.

Kathleen Hessert
Charlotte, NC 1998

Acknowledgments

While this book has been a labor of love for me, I can't take full credit for its completion. I owe a great deal of thanks to the people who sacrificed their time and energy to encourage, critique, enlighten and support my work and me.

Thanks go to my creative and energetic staff, especially Administrative Director Andrea Bowers and Marketing Director Rafi Shikoh. Their tireless efforts have made this book live up to the rigorous and professional standards of Sports Media Challenge.

Special thanks go to the enthusiastic sports professionals who shared their expertise with me by giving both feedback and encouragement. They include Mel Pulliam, Roger Valdiserri, George Raveling, and Mike Fresina. I also wish to acknowledge the contributions of Dr. Deborah A. Yow and Dr. William Bowden.

Foreword
Dr. Deborah A. Yow

Recently, a colleague of mine who is a NCAA Division I Athletic Director said to me: "With all of the other budgetary, compliance, personnel and competitive issues I face, there are times when media attention and scrutiny seem to come at my department in waves. We find ourselves running harder just to keep up." My colleague was simply overwhelmed with the responsibilities of being an AD, and didn't have the time and energy to handle the additional communication responsibilities that were being placed on him.

In an era in which media attention is focused on athletics in an intense and unparalleled manner, it's immensely important that coaches and athletic administrators understand the challenges and opportunities that they encounter when interfacing with almost everyone they come into contact with. This includes athletes, staff, athletic directors, sports information directors, colleagues, supporters, fans, the sports media, and others. Indeed, the success of any collegiate coach or athletic administrator rests in his or her ability to communicate and interact successfully with these groups.

These coaches and administrators shouldn't have to handle this immense responsibility alone. There are resources available to help them adapt to their new and changing roles. The organization that has offered the most effective training in this area is Sports Media Challenge.

Under the leadership of Kathleen Hessert, this company has made a national impact - training coaches, athletes and administrators to communicate effectively in their fields. I know this because of my firsthand experience with Kathleen and Sports Media Challenge. As the Athletic Director at the University of Maryland, I, along with our staff and coaches, have found the communication principles of Sports Media Challenge to be of substantial help to our athletic program.

I am delighted to give my endorsement to, and be a part of, this innovative and groundbreaking book. Because of the experience and expertise that has gone into its creation, *The Coach's Communication Playbook* is a valuable resource and will be an important tool for both coaches and administrators. It will equip athletics professionals to make the very most of their communication opportunities, and thereby enhance their standing. They'll also improve the standing of their team, department, organization or institution by candidly, proactively and wisely dealing with crucial situations.

The book also addresses the daunting challenge of prudently balancing the issues of privacy, confidentiality, and the appropriate timing of information release. These and many other relevant issues are explored in *The Coach's Communication Playbook*, in a concise and readily usable format.

You will find that this is one of the finest resources of its kind, and it'll assist you in developing the requisite skills for efficient, effective and professional communication.

Dr. Deborah A. Yow
Director of Athletics, University of Maryland
President-Elect, National Association of College Directors of Athletics
(2000-2001)
Member of the NCAA Management Council

Let's Get Started

My goal with The Coach's Communication Playbook is to help you develop into a communication champion. There's no doubt, better communicators are better coaches.

Kathleen Hessert
President, Sports Media Challenge

Introduction

Practice is running late and the head football coach sprints off the field, sweaty and still in his practice gear, to attend a small gathering of prominent alumni who have come to campus. A week ago, his AD asked him to attend while the coach was in the film room, engrossed in evaluating the opponent. He shows up unprepared and finds the president of the university is there, along with one of the world's most well-known stockbrokers, an astronaut, and a former U.S. Secretary of State - all of whom are formally dressed. They're prepared to donate millions to the school's academic programs and are also planning to help fund a new athletic complex.

Two weeks later, the school has gotten its academic scholarships, but the athletic department is still in its 60-year-old outdated building. The head coach still gets a cold stare from the AD every time he walks down the hall. Lack of communication and preparation for this one meeting may cost the coach his job, or at the very least, make for a miserable season.

This Can't Happen to Me!

Face it - this scenario could happen to any coach at any time. You may be the best in your field, work relentlessly, and have the trust of your staff - but if you aren't a powerful communicator, you will obscure your athletic successes.

We live in the "Communication Age." This doesn't just refer to faxes, email, the Internet, and all of the other technological advances we have made in the last few decades. It refers to people as well - people are expected to communicate more effectively than ever, and to do so in an informed, well-focused, concise, and even inspiring manner.

For some, this may require a whole new approach to communication; for others, simple refinement. This book was written to help you do just that. It's designed to be a valuable reference with practical applications and quick, easy-to-digest information.

What's Inside?

The Coach's Communication Playbook will teach you:

1 Ways to win at the media game.

2 How to maximize leadership through communication.

3 Tips for speaking in front of groups.

4 How to represent your team to outsiders.

5 Maximizing visibility and minimizing the risk.

6 What to do in crisis situations.

7 Ways to communicate with young athletes.

It also contains...

1 A chapter based on our *"Pocket Guide to Avoiding Misquotes."*

2 Quick, proven references such as *"D-Day Delivery Tips"* and *"The Nine Steps to Working a Crowd."*

3 Specialized worksheets and checklists that you can use over and over! Simply copy the pages and use them regularly, to help you keep track of your communication goals and improvement.

4 Internet resources and websites for quick reference.

5 An Appendix with additional resources and where to get them.

How to Locate the Information Inside:

In addition to the content, specific information is highlighted in one of four different categories:

STEP-BY-STEP

Easy to follow steps to help you develop a communication strategy.

PLAY-BY-PLAY

Detailed techniques to improve your communication skills.

POINTERS

Quick reminders in an easy-to-digest format.

WORKSHEET

A combination of quizzes, checklists and fill-in-the-blank forms to help you use the ideas covered in the previous chapter.

How to Use the Information Inside:

1 Try techniques in low risk situations first.

2 Adapt techniques to your individual style and the needs of your audience.

3 Keep it as a reference.

4 Use it to polish your skills before your presentation.

5 Copy the tips, pointers and worksheets to share with colleagues or friends.

PLAY BY PLAY

The Coach's Communication Role

To provide vision and direction.

To increase capabilities of team and team members.

To help with problems.

To create a supportive and results-oriented climate.

To provide resources and information.

To manage boundaries.

To remove barriers.

To challenge and push people out of their comfort zones.

To stay attuned to athlete's concerns.

To share the information and goals of the department with supervisors.

POINTERS

To Be a More Effective Coach:

Stress teamwork.

Promote trust and rapport.

Get feedback from your team.

Motivate your athletes.

Encourage task mastery.

Develop leadership.

Part 1

Speaking Skills: Presentation and Delivery

I am not one of those geniuses who can make a speech impromptu. I have made a great many happy impromptu speeches but I had time to prepare them.

Mark Twain

CHAPTER 1
Practice To Win

In the modern arena, *you can no longer rely on the same skills you used to. Although team policies rarely change and some coaches never update their playbooks, what does need to change is how you deliver necessary information to your team. Your athletes will probably tune out dry talks on policy, or other information that falls under that "general" heading, even though these are important topics they need to hear and remember. If you don't get these messages across the first time around, you'll find yourself repeating them all season - wasting time you may need practicing.*

Our world is overrun with soundbites and flash imagery which has created a generation of athletes who expect the same type of presentation from their teachers and coaches. Some days, you just don't want to think about presentation issues - but there's information of volume and importance that you have to get across. How, then, do you adjust? You can't give up, hoping that things work out for the best. The solution is to get the maximum out of your every word while making the most of your current skills and approach.

What Every Coach Should Ask Him/Herself

Before addressing your team, ask yourself these questions. Your answers will help you develop and enhance the necessary skills for effective team communication.

What information must they clearly understand when they leave this meeting?

How should I present these ideas in order to have the greatest impact?

Am I ready to answer questions? If not, how should I address them?

If there are questions, how do I end the meeting with a positive review of key points without starting over?

Do I need any follow-up or containment?

STEP BY STEP

Four Important Presentation Strategies

1 Focus
Sum up in one concise sentence what your meeting is about. Most audiences will walk away with only one major idea. You pick it! For example, if you have to address the team about a mid season discipline problem, open with one finely focused sentence. "This meeting will address athletes who are skipping class and how it affects the entire team."

2 Purpose
Expand on that focus statement and think about the purpose of calling the team together. What do you want the team to know? What do you want them to think about after the meeting?

3 Timing
As in every sport, the timing of a meeting is critical. A clear message delivered in a timely manner will keep the rumor mill from spinning out of control. For example, if one of your athletes has decided to leave the team, ask yourself: Is it best to announce it as soon as you know? If you don't, will misinformation spread as to why he or she is leaving?

4 Position
If you're making an announcement, understand your team's possible position. Again, ask yourself: Do they already know what you're presenting? Is there an information leak? How strong are the rumors? Who already knows (i.e., parents, media, student body)? and, What's been done to contain it? Does your team already have opinions on the subject? Keeping their thoughts and reactions in mind will keep you from sending the wrong message.

"Off the Cuff"

You won't always have time to plan a presentation for a team meeting. So much in sports happens "off the cuff." But there are ways to give those impromptu talks without sounding like you needed more time to plan out what to say. Follow this simple formula for preparation and your "off the cuff" comments will come across as if you had days to prepare.

Quick Prep Technique

As issues come up that you need to address with your team, quickly divide these issues into one of the following categories:

LOW   MEDIUM   HIGH

Once you rank an issue you will know how much time you need to prepare. You won't prepare the same way for a LOW profile communication situation, as you will for a HIGH profile one.

What Your Audience Takes Away

By using what little lead-time you have to prepare a message that will have the highest impact possible, you'll be a successful speaker a greater percentage of the time. Preparation allows you to dictate the result. You'll be able to answer the most important question: What do I want them to do with this information? For example, as you go over team policies, identify what results you want and how to obtain them. When you're able to deliver a clear message, you'll ultimately build a team that trusts itself and you!

How People Receive Information

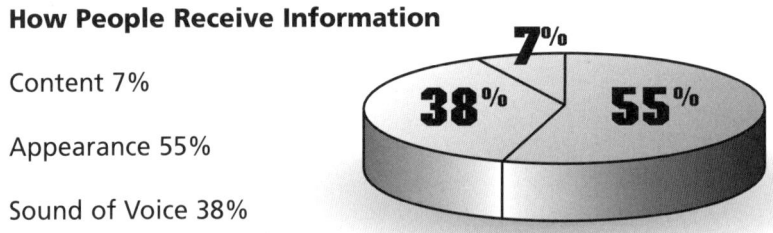

Content 7%

Appearance 55%

Sound of Voice 38%

Consistency in your message helps make your content shine.

In face-to-face communication, 93% of your effectiveness rests on how you look and sound. Only 7% of your credibility is derived from your content. On the telephone, 80% of your credibility is based on the way you sound, 20% is based on content. When there's inconsistency in your message, people believe what they see more than anything else.

Bottom Line: Perception is reality.

When you look, sound and speak a message of confidence and control, people will believe you.

CHAPTER 2
Valuable Presentation Skills

As much as you'd like to focus on practice, conditioning and strategy, you know there's a lot more to the coach's job. Part of being a coach means speaking in front of a variety of people for a variety of reasons.

Being a skilled communicator is even more critical now than it was in the past. You're looked at to speak to a variety of groups (including the media), raise funds, negotiate between athletes and your organization, and produce a quality team that can win. While you may have the best record in the state, you'll still be judged to a great extent on how well you speak and how persuasive you are.

That's why it's critical, each time you speak, that you sell your ideas to your audience and that they buy in. You must connect both intellectually and emotionally with your audience, using one to reinforce the other. In other words, you must speak to their hearts as well as their heads. You'll make more of an impact that way!

Who Wants You?

Some of the groups you'll be asked to address include:

Your Team	Community Officials
Fan Groups	Student Groups & Organizations
The Media	Alumni
Faculty	Financial supporters

High School Students and their Parents

Athletic Department Personnel or School Administrators

People Who've Hired You to Speak at an Event

Sponsors (Such as apparel or equipment companies.)

Four Presentation Skills to Master

1 Prepare Yourself
Take time to think about what you need to say, then say it out loud! What you think in your mind or write on paper doesn't always sound the same when you say it. If you can, practice saying your message to someone else, then ask him/her what you said. If they can't restate your message clearly, you're not getting through.

2 KISS or "Keep It Simple, Stupid!"
When writing something to be spoken, use short and simple sentences. It'll confuse your audience if sentences are long and complicated. Again, practice saying it out loud to make sure it sounds right.

3 One Theme Only
Pick the focus of your presentation and stick to it. Content should be used to reinforce your key point. You should be able to state your focus in one sentence. Ask yourself, What one thing do I want them to remember when they leave?

If your goal is to get donations from support groups, then the focus of the presentation may be: What we could accomplish with more money? or How you can help our team with donations?

4 Know Your Audience
Your language is very different in the locker room than it is at a banquet. Keep that in mind before you make any presentation. Remember that you're speaking for your audience, not yourself, so gear the message to them.

When you go into a presentation without a clearly defined and well-supported message it leaves athletes, parents, or supporters unsure of what you're asking of them.

You may have to change your style of language, length, or type of content to better fit your audience. Be willing to do this - it makes you a lot more effective. Find out as many details about the group you're talking to and customize your presentation accordingly. Encouraging young athletes to "Win One for the Gipper" may convince them that you're crazy. But incorporating that phrase for an older audience will probably get their attention.

Do some research to familiarize yourself with the organization or group and find out who's in it. Also, make sure you know the correct pronunciation of the organization's name beforehand.

POINTERS ⮕

Get to Know Your Audience Beforehand

1 Who are they?
Names, Ages, Genders, Affiliations

2 What is their background?
Education/Experience Level, Economic Status, Special Interests

3 What do they expect of you?
Information, Understanding/Empathy, Action

4 Will they be receptive...
To You? To Your Message?

Keep it Positive, Grab Them and Never Let Them See You Sweat

In every way possible, be as positive as your purpose and message will allow. People are always more moved by a positive message.

Get the attention of your audience immediately and they'll want to listen. The best way to do this is by telling the audience what they all want to know: What's in it for me? or *WIIFM*. (Pronounced: "WHIFF-um." It sounds silly, but it'll help you to remember.)

Often, by combining what your audience wants to hear with what you want them to know is the best place to start. It gives them a reason to listen further rather than tune you out. For example: If you're speaking to parents who want to know how successful the team will be and you're in a transitional year, you may try a direct answer.

Example:

How good are we this year?

"Well, we are in transition, which is interesting because we don't know what will happen."

The cliche still holds true. No matter how hopeless things may feel, keep a poker face. Nervousness is natural, but you need to learn to control it and make it work for you. Don't let the stress show through. Also, don't draw attention to mistakes during your presentation. If you keep going, chances are that no one will notice problems.

A seamless presentation starts when you enter a room. Don't rush in. Take your time, breathe normally, relax and look around. A few moments of silence will allow you to gather your thoughts, and it also draws the audience in. Focus only on the positive before/during the presentation. Animation of movement, gesture, and voice all signal to the audience that you're certain of yourself. Controlled body language is important - **practice it**.

PLAY BY PLAY

The Basics of Speaking to Groups

1 Maintain eye contact.

2 Look at audience members - not the tops of their heads.

3 Avoid darting or scanning eyes.

4 Hold contact with an audience member for 3-5 seconds, then move on.

5 Avoid podiums. Instead, move deliberately and use gestures - it shows the audience that you're certain of yourself.

Presentation and Delivery

A Few Extras

You can add visuals to your presentation - things like videos, graphics, even a diagram on a black board. The use of pictures with words will increase understanding by up to 200%! Narrow your message to a single theme and write it for them to see. If the audience tunes out, they're likely to focus on your visual.

Make sure you use audiovisuals that are appropriate to your message and that you're comfortable using them. That means you must practice your presentation with the visuals to make sure it runs smoothly. Avoid overkill - you can overuse visuals to the point of tedium. Remember that we're a society of scanners.

Closing Statements

Give as much thought to the closing of your presentation as you do to the opening. Be sure to briefly restate your central theme. Use the end of your presentation to set the mood you want listeners to take away. *Is there a memorable story or phrase to sum up your focused presentation?* The end is what they'll remember. Leave the audience with your agenda, not theirs.

The Final Test... "Q & A": Use It to Your Advantage

Just when you thought it was safe to leave the stage... Wham. It's time for questions. But don't be afraid - this can be an opportunity for spontaneous humor, so relax and have fun. Questions aren't a threat to your message; they're just another way to deliver it. With just a few tips, you can turn a Q & A session into a powerful communication tool.

Each answer should be a mini-speech with a beginning, middle and end. You don't have to answer every question in lengthy detail, so once you've devoted enough time to Q & A, feel free to end the session. After questions, take a moment to refocus your audience. If you leave the room at the close of questions, it's the last question, not your message that they'll remember. Therefore, always restate your focus. Leave the audience with your agenda, not theirs.

PLAY BY PLAY

Choreograph a Well-Controlled, Productive Q&A Session

1 Practice "Bridging."
Answer *their questions*, then refocus by bridging to *your message*.

2 Don't repeat negatives.
Repetition reinforces the negative. Reword the question if necessary.

3 Strategically move around the room to promote or prohibit questions.

4 Intentionally include and exclude audience members effectively through the use of eye contact.
In other words, if you want to shut off questions, look away from the problem questioner.

Q & A Control

Walter Cronkite once said, "There are no bad questions, only bad answers." If you've been subject to seemingly stupid questions, that may be hard to believe. Here's how not to give a bad answer by maintaining control of the situation:

The ABC's to Responding to Challenging Comments

The ABC's are a powerful tool for dealing with a challenging and *antagonistic* audience.

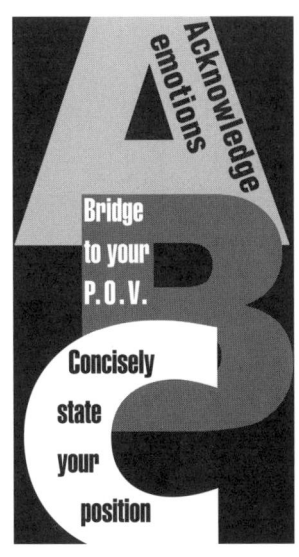

Acknowledge Emotions
Recognize and acknowledge their emotional position before moving on. In other words, *listen to them* before going further. They've a right to their opinion, and you need to acknowledge that. You don't have to agree with it.

Bridge to Your Point of View
Transition to your point of view with an easy phrase like, "However, when we look at this another way..." or "The key issue here seems to be..." With this technique, you demonstrate respect for their perspective while putting emphasis on your own.

Concisely State Your Opinion
Clearly and concisely state your point of view. More words don't necessarily mean more impact.

[Based on the popular laminated reference card **"The ABC's to Responding to Challenging Comments"** available from **Sports Media Challenge**.]

POINTERS ➔

Make the Best of Q&A

1 Anticipate difficult questions and practice the answers beforehand.

2 Listen carefully to each question.

3 Correct misstatements and other misinformation.

4 Stay cool, tactful, personable and compassionate.

4 Admit it when you don't know something.

4 Treat each answer as a mini-speech.

CHAPTER 3
How to Motivate

Notre Dame's former head coach Lou Holtz would ask his team, "Who in here wants to be great? Stand up." *Obviously, the whole team would stand up. For the rest of the season, Holtz would hold athletes accountable by reminding them of this meeting. Holtz would say, "You guys told me you wanted to be great, I'm only doing what you said you wanted."*

Coach Holtz had a way of doing things that caused athletes to be self-motivational, instead of trying to motivate the whole team by himself. That was his approach, but there are many other approaches out there. You have to pick what works for you, but keep in mind you can't always rely on tactics that *used* to work. Remember that you can never lose sight of your team values and team issues when motivating.

For years, coaches have felt the need to "selectively motivate" based on competition and team chemistry. Now, however, with great upsets such as the NBA lockout of 1998 and a sports environment in which athletes are moved primarily by their own success, it's time to take another look at motivation and its place in the locker room as well as on the sidelines.

Motivational Tactics That Don't Work

1 "Win one for the Gipper"

This phrase is no longer the great motivating tool it once was. Most athletes today don't even recognize it. In other words, look to *their* generation of star athletes for stories to inspire them.

2 The Coach who Cried Wolf

Coaches concede that you can't always be the source of your team's motivation. Sure, you can occasionally call on history and sentimentality to pull a team together for a big event, but seasons are comprised of events both big and small. Coaches who dig into their motivational bag of tricks too many times will end up receiving the "boy who cried wolf" reaction from athletes.

Motivational Tools That Do Work

Make it Personal

Identify what it is that will make your team want to play to win. While some people more readily accept that there's no "I" in team, other individuals may need personal pushing. You can motivate a team with different interests by making *your* goal the one thing they all have in common.

Paint Pictures With Your Words

Develop a theme and communicate your ideas clearly. Keep your desired result clearly in sight. Show your team what to do, don't just tell them.

Use Quotes or Anecdotes

Help athletes get a picture of what you want. Be creative and current. Telling a team today to storm the beach at Normandy won't be as effective now as it was in the 1960's. Your athletes will relate better to stories from their own generation, such as the Northwestern Football Program of the 90's - a program that went from the doghouse to the Rose Bowl.

Always Think About What You're Saying

They want to know - *What's in it for me?* and *Why should I care?* Remind athletes of their individual roles and how they relate to your overall goal.

Promote Involvement

Ask select team members questions that lead to your goal. If you've already presented your theme, you can easily ask an athlete: *What do you consider to be the most important ingredient to the team's success?* You should get the answer you want!

Change the Setting

It's not always possible to change where your team meets, but you can change where they sit. This is very effective. It can give your words, even if they're repetitive, a refreshing boost. It will also give your audience a new perspective, and encourage response. For example, try putting chairs in a circle or U-shape to encourage interaction. If you're in a place where the chairs don't move, such as an auditorium, encourage them to sit in the first few rows.

Watch That Temper...

When you lose your cool, you lose control. While many believe that the spontaneous tirade is the staple of the motivational talk, it isn't always effective and can even be counterproductive. If your motivation is to have a long lasting impact, your talk must be thought out, controlled and something you can clearly repeat when a reminder is necessary.

Using Motivational Visuals

Visuals back up what you're saying. This is very important, because most people forget what they hear in 24 hours. Things like graphs, blackboards, pictures, and videotape help you as a speaker too. The visuals take the focus off you. Also, keep in mind that many of your athletes are probably visual learners, which means they'll get more from video and graphics than they'll get from just hearing you talk.

Visual Impact:

Improves your credibility and leadership.

Increases the audience's comprehension and retention.

Increases agreement.

Increases the probability of action.

CHAPTER 4
Delivery

As you've no doubt heard before, how you say something is often as important as what you say. This is where **stage presence** becomes important. If your voice, body language, and gestures aren't in agreement with your words, then your audience will lose your message. Imagine watching a nervous coach addressing his or her team with head down, voice uneven, and hands fidgeting at his or her sides. Even if you're giving great news to your team, they're likely to leave the meeting feeling dissatisfied and uninformed.

POINTERS →

When Speaking to an Audience, Don't...

1 Rush your speech.

2 Say you're nervous.

3 Apologize.

4 Let your eyes dance.

5 Fidget.

6 Look at the ceiling or the floor.

7 Panic.

Part

1

Presentation and Delivery

PLAY BY PLAY

D-Day Delivery Tips

1 Begin your presentation without referring to your notes.

2 Speak loudly and clearly enough to be heard, but not too rapidly.

3 Maintain flexibility - keep a pulse on your audience, and change course when necessary.

4 Avoid fillers such as "like," "um," and "you know."

5 Stand on the balls of your feet for a dynamic presence. Don't lean.

6 Keep it short. "An example is better than a sermon."

7 Look at your audience and smile, you're both happy to be there.

8 Talk to the audience members, one at a time. Look at individual's eyes.

9 Use colorful nouns and "kicking" verbs. Use your words to show, not tell.

10 When receiving an award, keep it in full view of the audience at all times. Use it to enhance your acceptance speech, not in place of it.

11 When finished, move out with confidence.

D-Day, or Delivery Day

Remember your Boy or Girl Scout days and the motto "Be Prepared?" Well, you're going to need it when it's time to speak in front of a group. Know what you're going to say before you arrive, and jot down your organized ideas (not word for word) in outline form on a notepad or index card.

Using Body Language

No, body language isn't something people look for in a pickup bar. It's a powerful tool to aid you in getting your message across.

Position Yourself for Success

	POWERFUL	POWERLESS	DISASTROUS
EYE CONTACT	Direct eyes; talking and listening.	Avoiding direct eye contact.	Staring, glaring "looking down on."
FACIAL EXPRESSION	Congruent with verbal messages.	Incongruent (i.e., smiling while angry).	Lifted eyebrow, pursed lips, squinting.
POSTURE	Erect, energized, comfortable.	Slouched, no energy, immobile.	Rigid, "puffed up" chest.
VOICE	Clear, evenly paced, well projected.	Too slow, too low, pitch goes up at end of sentence.	Loud, demanding, too fast to be understood.
BODY MOVEMENT & GESTURES	Minimal, deliberate, used to add emphasis to verbal message.	Too many gestures, fidgeting, touching face, hair, mouth.	Pointing finger, broad gestures, movement that violates others' personal space.

CHAPTER 5
Setting the Stage

So much energy goes into your speech, materials, and visuals, that it's easy to overlook one of the most important aspects of your presentation - your **entrance.** The first few moments of your presentation, when you take center stage, are some of the most crucial moments. It doesn't matter where you are or what you're talking about; your audience's first impression will directly influence your overall effectiveness. So, whether you're speaking to a bunch of sweaty athletes in a gym or standing on a stage in front of a thousand people, make sure those first moments shed a positive light on the rest of your presentation.

Another important moment in your presentation occurs before you set foot on stage. It's your introduction - the few crucial bits of information about you that lets the audience know who you are. How will you be represented? It's up to you to take control of the introduction so that your entrance and presentation are as powerful as possible.

Use the pointers in this chapter to help you prepare your introduction and entrance. The more you prepare in advance, the less you will have to worry about the day of the event.

Making a Dazzling Entrance

"Attention grabbers are very important in a talk; you can't get them to make the trip with you, if you never get them to the airport!"
T. Bubba Bechtol; Humorist, CSP, NSA, SAG

The following is an example of one of Bechtol's attention-grabbing entrances. While his approach may be gutsier than many coaches feel comfortable with, keep it in mind as an example when you want to make a creative and high impact entrance.

Also, remember: *tailor your entrance to fit your topic.* Never use a lighthearted introduction when you have a serious topic, or vice versa.

Get Their Attention and Make Them Understand

A few years ago, he was asked to speak to the *American Medical Association* on leadership training. He wanted to grab their attention, and since they were doctors, he was unsure of their interest in his topic. This is what he did:

Bubba went to the meeting planner and told her that he was going to do something odd immediately after his introduction. This made her very curious and upset, so he told her to trust him and not to interrupt anything on stage. She just threw up her hands and said, "Okay, Bubba!"

After he was introduced, he walked out on stage to address 5,000 doctors. He walked up to the mike and started to say something, cut it off, put his hand on his chin, looked at them thoughtfully for a moment, and said: "Excuse me for just a moment!" He then turned and walked off the stage.

No one did anything; they just sat there waiting for what was to happen next. The meeting planner thought Bubba had lost his mind!

He waited two minutes, four, then five, and the crowd began to murmur and shift in their seats. The air got very thick. At six minutes, the meeting planner was in his face, screaming "do something!" He waited until the first few people began to get up and leave, then at nearly 10 minutes, he walked up to the microphone. He paused until they began to sit back down, waited a long minute or so just looking at them, and then said in a loud clear voice . . . "How does that feel?"

Stunned silence met his words, until they began to get it. After a few chuckles from those doctors that understood right away, he said, "I had another speech to attend to at the back of the stage!"

They roared with laughter for five minutes, and just as they were quieting down, he brought a box of 5-to-10 year old magazines and began to throw them out into the group, yelling: "Hey, read these until he can get back with you!" They fought over those magazines like they were dollar bills!

After the Entrance

At the point where he regained control over the meeting, he went on to give his talk on "being professional." He emphasized the fact that doctors can forget that - in the lifesaving profession they're in - it's important to recognize people when they're waiting for them, no matter how busy they are.

It's important that you, too, take control of your audience after making an entrance. In other words, grab their attention and keep it! Don't allow your entrance to detract from the validity of your topic.

Preparing Your Introduction

Imagine that you're about to speak to a crowded room, and the announcer begins his/her introduction by saying, "Our company has spent millions updating our computer system so it's state of the art, and we've spent millions more to improve our facilities. Now, all we have to do is improve you! Here's Coach "X" to help us accomplish that."

This actually happened, and no doubt with that kind of introduction, the speaker had a hard time motivating the audience. How willingly do you think they'll accept your message? Chances are, you'll end up spending most of your time digging your way out of hole the introducer put you in, trying to convince the audience that they shouldn't resent you. The best way to ensure a great introduction or biographical sketch is to write it yourself - or have someone write it for you. Use the plan on the next page when preparing your introduction for the big day.

Part

1

Presentation and Delivery

STEP BY STEP

How to Prepare

1 Test your introduction out on friends and family. Ask yourself: *Do they want to learn more? Are they anticipating your message?*

2 Send your introduction to the organization sponsoring your appearance ahead of time. It's preferable to have your secretary or Sports Information Director send it, because it'll be more readily accepted if it comes from someone other than yourself.

3 Request that they use your piece to introduce you at the podium, and if at all possible, talk to the person giving the introduction. Make sure they have the pronunciation of your name straight, and go over important factors, such as the history of your team. What is obviously important to you may be disregarded by someone else, such as the fact that your team went to the "Orange Bowl" not the "Citrus Bowl."

4 Update your introduction to include recent events (i.e., you led your team to the National Championship for the x time in x years). And lastly, as a precautionary step, make sure you bring a copy of your introduction to the actual event. There's a very good chance it has been lost in the mass of details. There's nothing worse than an introduction that's thrown together 5 minutes before you're scheduled to speak.

The Components of A Successful Introduction

By using the following steps, you'll be sure to satisfy the overall goals of a successful introduction - to generate interest and anticipation with the audience by giving them a glimpse of the "man/woman behind the legend."

POINTERS➔

A Successful Introduction Can Touch On:

1 Your coaching or personal style/approach.

2 Your voice - *Is there something unusual about it?*

3 Your physical characteristics - *What makes you stand out?*

4 Your values - *What do you care about?*

5 Quotes from a person valued by the audience. This needs to be someone who can make an impact with the audience members.

6 Quotes from others about you.

7 Professional and personal highlights.

8 Community involvement or charitable service.

Remember that a good introduction sets the stage for you and stacks things in your favor. On the other hand, if the introduction is substandard, you can waste all of your time trying to recover from it. Read over these tips when preparing your introduction. You won't need to use all of the suggestions, especially since one of the main essentials of an introduction is to *keep it short.*

Use the previous pointers to create a powerful and effective introduction. Then, to test the power of your introduction, use the criteria on the following page to evaluate it.

Part

1

Presentation and Delivery

STEP BY STEP

A Powerful Introduction Will...

1 Act as a bridge between the speaker and the presentation topic and the audience.

2 Generate excitement about the speaker and the upcoming presentation.

3 Establish the speaker as a credible source.

4 Help the speaker feel at home and lighten audience resistance.

5 Express thanks to the audience and acknowledge the worth of the presentation.

6 Be brief. One or two minutes should be enough time to say the things that need to be said. When constructing the intro, think "highlights."

Disastrous Announcements - The Intro to Your Intro

As a reminder, when you get there be sure to ask the introducer what announcements, if any, are going to be made before you speak. If, for example, you find out that they intend to announce that one of the organization's valued members has suddenly passed away, the news will definitely put a pall over the audience and make entertaining them difficult, if not impossible. If you're faced with an announcement that threatens your presentation, request that they don't make the announcement before your presentation. This can drastically affect the mood of your audience.

If something like this happens despite your efforts, realize that you have to speak to the audience's current emotional level. If they're in a serious mood after the announcement, you must address them in a serious manner when you take the stage. The opposite also applies - if an announcement generates laughter and amusement in the audience right before you're supposed to speak about a serious topic; this can create problem for you also.

A speaker was once scheduled to deliver a humorous speech to a group of 150 executives. It was just about time to start when it was announced that the space shuttle Challenger had exploded, and the astronauts were presumed dead. After such an announcement, the speaker had to make a quick decision. He discarded his humorous approach, and instead matched the serious mood of the audience. He then gradually lifted the mood until he was able to deliver his message appropriately.

The key is to get their attention by matching the mood they're in when you take the stage. Once you've captured their attention, gradually take them to the emotional level of your speech. After a devastating announcement, you may never be able to use the funny stories you had prepared, but at least you can lighten the mood and deliver your message without alienating your audience.

CHAPTER 6
Attention-Grabbing Content

Presentation and Delivery

Though most audiences expect to be bored, they hope that this time they'll be wrong. Therefore, when you prepare to speak in front of a group, you need to spend a lot of time thinking about what you want to say. It's not always easy to prepare a talk that will grab the attention of your audience, but it can be fun if you get creative. This chapter offers some easy tips to help you develop content that's both informative and entertaining, using techniques like humor and storytelling. Use these techniques in your presentations, but also use them for other kinds of communication. It will make communication more enjoyable for you and those you come into contact with!

Using Humor to Build Interest

Some coaches are reluctant to use humor with young athletes, because they expect to be taken seriously. They're concerned that humor will undermine the respect and authority they've worked so hard to get.

However, when used appropriately, humor can be a powerful motivational and communication tool. Athletes often feel more comfortable around people with a fun side to them. When it's time to be serious, be serious - but when an opportunity arises to throw a little humor into your conversation, try it!

Humor is great for a presentation, but it can and should be used in your day-to-day communications as well. Remember - sports are supposed to be fun! Humor helps you and your team diffuse stress, learn more readily, and just plain enjoy yourselves.

PLAY BY PLAY

Where Do You Find Humor?

1 Look around yourself for funny situations, stories, etc.

2 Think Funny! Once you lighten your mood, funny ideas are more likely to pop into your head.

3 Think of silly or absurd everyday situations that your audience can relate to.

4 Catalogue humor - keep track of funny things you think of, so that you can develop them into funny stories later.

5 Look to outside sources such as books or magazines. For quick reference, check out some humor websites with jokes and humorous quotations.

Relax!

Most people today are so stressed out that humor is being taught in corporate America as a coping tool. When used appropriately, humor relieves pressure and helps everyone relax. You can lighten up the intensity of a difficult situation, and build camaraderie between yourself and your athletes.

Grab Their Attention

A lot of people think you have to open with a joke. Wrong - this technique is typically meant to loosen up the speaker more than the audience. However, interesting information and humor *within your presentation* increase the value of what you're saying. Athletes are far more likely to listen to you after you've gotten their attention with a humorous anecdote. Jokes, on the other hand, are usually old and need a stand-up comic not a coach to tell them effectively.

POINTERS ➔

Ways to Lighten Up

1 Tell stories instead of jokes.

2 Use humorous visuals or props.

3 Turn everyday situations into funny anecdotes.

4 Let your natural sense of humor shine through.

Part 1

Presentation and Delivery

Use Funny Stories

Coach Charlie Spoonhour, the head basketball coach at St. Louis University, tells the story of a time that he was accidentally locked in a locker room during half time while his team was playing in the NCAA tournament.

When he was discovered and let out, the very apologetic woman who released him tried to show him how to use the doorknob. He responded: "Lady, I don't have time for 'Door 101.'" Instead of chastising her, he made a hero out of her for rescuing him by sharing the story with anyone who would listen.

Later in the tournament, when his team was losing badly, Spoonhour asked: "Why didn't you lock me up today?"

This story illustrates how Spoonhour used a humorous story from a real life situation to enhance his communications. This example works on several levels: first, he turned a negative situation into a positive one using humor when he was initially locked in. Then, he relieved the pressure of a difficult situation when his team was losing by asking her the ironic question "Why didn't you lock me up today?" Finally, he used the story later on, both as an example and as a humorous anecdote that was uniquely his. He also realized that poking fun at yourself makes everyone more approachable.

STEP BY STEP

Find Your *Style* of Humor

Answering the questions below will help determine the type of humor that fits your style of speaking or writing.

1 What is your purpose when you speak or write? To entertain? To teach? To motivate? To inform? To question? Are you supposed to be hilarious or at least slightly funny?

2 Can your humorous material be only mildly amusing or must it be drop-dead funny? Do you want your audiences to burst out laughing, smile, or nod in agreement when you tell a story?

3 Who will generally be in your audience? Families? All men? All women? Teenagers? Elderly? Young people?

4 Will your audiences appreciate slightly risqué illustrations? (Look out, you're treading on thin ice here.)

5 What image do you want your material to portray? That you're a nice human being? A sarcastic individual? A down-home Southerner? A successful businessperson?

6 Do you tell jokes well? Do you deliver long stories better than you do one-liners?

7 Do you ad lib well? Must every story be memorized word for word?

8 Can your material revolve around you, your family, and your experiences, or do you prefer to steer away from personal references?

9 Do you feel comfortable poking fun at yourself?

[Adapted from Jeanne Robertson's *Don't Let the Funny Stuff Get Away*[1]. This book is the best resource to help someone think and talk "funny." It will help those of you who have a strong sense of humor and want to improve it, and those of you who are humorously impaired and want to build your humor savvy.]

Stomach-Grabbing Humor Websites

These sites have a lot of information - jokes, stories, and parodies - usually organized by subject. The content varies in taste and quality, so filter what you use very carefully. Even if you don't use anything you find at these sites, you will enjoy a good chuckle!

General Humor:
Jokes, anecdotes, one-liners, and more.

Funny Town - http://www.funnytown.com

Grady Jim's Humor Site - http://www.gradyjim.com

Brad Templeton's *Rec.Humor.Funny* - http://www.netfunny.com/rhf

Idea Bank (Note: there's a subscription fee) - http://www.idea-bank.com/

Oracle Humor Archives - http://www.oraclehumor.com

Sports Humor Sites:
Jokes are organized by sport. Quality varies.

T'NT Sports Humor Archive -
http://www.nb.net/~tntcoll/humor.htm

Jock Brains at Ergonomica -
http://ergonomica.com/funmail/html/jockbrains.html

Sport Jokes and Humor -
http://www.geocities.com/~1rodney/sports.html

Have Fun, But Watch What You Say

While humor is a great way to grab their attention, don't go to inappropriate extremes. Avoid at all costs using foul language or ethnic slurs and no matter how funny they are, don't tell racist or sexist jokes. Remember: if you've made just one person in your audience uncomfortable, you've gone too far.

STEP BY STEP

Nine Steps to Developing Your Stories

1 Message
Decide what specific message you want to convey.

2 Examples
Recall examples that illustrate your message.

3 Characters
Recall three people (or less) who were affected by the example. These are your characters.

4 Turning Point
Find one event that triggered the action. This is the turning point.

5 Payoff
List how your characters were affected or what they learned as a result of the turning point. This is the pay-off of the story.

6 Setup
Describe what your characters knew or how they acted prior to the turning point. This is the setup of the story.

7 Plot
Link the setup, turning point and payoff. This is the plot of your story.

8 Tie-in Question
Ask a tie-in question that relates your story to your listeners and leads them closer to the specific message you want them to leave with.

9 Point
Make sure your story has a point that's as sharp as can be. Is its message obviously relevant to your objectives?

[From Story Selling™ by Dr. Paul Homily. For more information see Appendix page 167]

Use Storytelling to Create an Impact

One of the mantras of professional speakers today is **"Make a point, tell a story."** The reason that this technique is so widely used and respected is because it works. Your audience needs to hear your stories for several reasons.

First of all, a story can serve as an example to back up your point. Imagine that you have to gather your team to go over some important new regulations. If you simply recite the new regulations, you'll lose their attention. But if you tell the story of a mishap that occurred before the regulation took effect, they'll be more likely to remember.

Secondly, a story will break up the monotony of facts that you have to deliver. It breaks the boredom for you and your athletes.

Finally, you can develop a "signature story," one that people will associate with you. This will help people to remember you, and you'll find that if it's a good one, people will begin to request it. Use the following tips to develop your storytelling talent.

Collecting and Using Your Stories

Stories have a powerful impact on your listeners. However, before you can use them to persuade, entertain or gain appropriate attention, you have to recognize a story in the making and then have it prepared when you need it.

How to Collect and Use Stories:

Look out for good stories.

Many small and insignificant situations have a lesson that may apply to your various messages and audiences. Always be observant and cross-reference your daily experiences to how they relate to a particular message.

Collect and file interesting stories.

Write all the interesting stories you can think of, and put them in different categories. Unless you write them down, the stories will be forgotten. You can divide these into the following categories: *theme* (perseverance, determination, etc.), *sport* (basketball, football, swimming, soccer, etc.), *age group* (young athletes, parents, etc.), or *level of experience.*

Find places to use them.

By using these stories in different situations you'll also test them for their effectiveness and be able to refine them.

Use analogies.

These are mini-stories that bring your message to life. Be observant and keep track of these analogies and then relate them to different situations. Write them down and use them often to evaluate their effectiveness.

Identify how a story applies to your Audiences.

This includes obvious (team) and non-obvious (parents, administration, business executives, etc.) audiences. This will help you identify the right stories for your different audiences.

CHAPTER 7
Bringing It All Together

The 8 Steps to Speaking in Front of Groups

Use these steps when speaking to groups such as teams, fan groups, alumni, and the media.

1 Put into one sentence the main message that the audience must walk away with. It improves focus and the listeners' chances of remembering your most important idea.

2 Tailor your message to the audience. Craft comments to answer:
   a) *What does it mean to them?*
   b) *Why should they care?*
   c) *Does it pass the "so what" test?*

3 Organize your ideas to support the theme, ensure a good flow, and appropriately allocate time for each subtopic.

4 Craft your opening and closing statements to grab attention and reinforce the message.

5 Look at individuals, not the audience as a whole. Hold eye contact 3-5 seconds before moving on to someone else. Make eye contact with as many people as possible, without obvious eye shifting.

6 Increase your energy output with larger audiences. Think of yourself as a light bulb: the larger the room and the audience, the higher the wattage. Speaking in front of a small group requires three times the energy used when talking one-on-one. Additional energy is needed for impact with larger groups.

7 Gesture for greater impact. Reach away from your body to be more powerful, visible, and for greater variety. Link gestures to spoken ideas. Don't use repetitive or meaningless gestures or phrases.

8 Physically command the room - it's your stage! Move strategically to redirect nervous energy. Avoid podiums. Stand tall and strong. You and your message are their real purpose for being there.

Part
1

Presentation and Delivery

WORKSHEET

Speaking Worksheet - Preparation

If your goal is to give an outstanding presentation, you should be answering "yes" to the following questions. If you haven't answered "yes" to all of them this time, don't give up! Keep this worksheet to mark your improvement.

Theme
What is your theme?

_____

_____

How can you best articulate and emphasize the theme throughout the presentation?

_____

_____

_____

Audience Customization
Who exactly is your audience?

_____

What do you know about the sponsoring organization?

_____

_____

_____

Within your content, do you answer:
*What does this message mean to
the audience?*   Yes   No

Why should they care?   Yes   No

WORKSHEET

Speaking Worksheet - Preparation con't

What does the audience expect from you?

_____

_____

_____

*Have you incorporated those expectations
into your presentation?*   Yes   No

*Have you provided an appropriate balance
of fact and insight?*   Yes   No

Impact Elements
*Do you have a high impact opening to your
presentation that will immediately capture
the audience's attention?*   Yes   No

*Have you crafted a high impact closing
statement that sets the departing mood?*   Yes   No

*Do you clearly state the action you want
taken for each major content segment?*   Yes   No

*Have you anticipated all negative, positive,
and obvious questions and planned answers
for them?*   Yes   No

*Have you decided what information you
will delete if necessary?*   Yes   No

WORKSHEET

Speaking Worksheet - Preparation con't

Rehearsal

Have you rehearsed the presentation
out loud?   Yes   No

Have you rehearsed with your visual aids?   Yes   No

Have you practiced in front of others for
candid feedback?   Yes   No

Have you timed and evaluated the
presentation more than once for accuracy?   Yes   No

Environment Checklist

❑ Check the room you're presenting in at least
45 minutes before you speak. Stand looking at the
stage, seeing what your audience will see.
Can you see well enough?

❑ Check the room lights. They should be bright
enough for you to be able to see the entire audience
without washing out your visual aids.

❑ Personally check out your audiovisual equipment
before you start the meeting.

❑ What kind of microphone will you use? Check it out
before you face the audience. Will the microphone
system allow you to move about the room?

❑ Do you have hand-held microphones for the
audience, to promote questions and comments?

❑ Do you have a pointing device available, if needed,
for your visuals?

WORKSHEET

Speaking Worksheet - Preparation con't

Notes:

_____

_____

_____

_____

_____

_____

_____

_____

_____

_____

_____

_____

_____

_____

_____

_____

_____

_____

_____

_____

_____

_____

_____

_____

_____

_____

_____

_____

_____

_____

_____

Part
1

Presentation and Delivery

Part 2

Speaking Skills: Interpersonal Communication

Great teamwork is the only way
to reach our ultimate moments,
to create the breakthroughs
that define our careers,
to fulfill our lives with a
sense of lasting significance.

Pat Riley
President and Head Coach, Miami Heat

CHAPTER 8
One-On-One Situations

Whether you're comfortable with it or not, your athletes look to you not only for guidance regarding their sport, but for advice about non-sports related issues. There's a very good chance that an athlete will come to you to talk about a problem or look for some advice, whether it's personal or team related.

Parents may also come to you to discuss their child's sports and overall performance. Effective one-on-one communication skills will help you to better handle these situations, no matter how uncomfortable they can sometimes get.

Two-Way Communication

Open communication between you and your athletes or their parents will help you to recognize and eliminate barriers that separate both parties. Communication is always more effective when people believe it flows two ways. In other words, let them know that your door is always open to discuss problems they have.

Sometimes, all the person needs is a sounding board, and being a good listener helps you build trust with your athletes. So when you hear that knock on your door, remember that being a good listener will help you establish a better relationship with them as people and competitors.

You might not want to hear about an athlete's personal problems, but remember that an athlete cannot perform optimally if his or her mind is on those problems. Athletes will come to you because you're an authority figure they look up to. Their parents will come to you for the same reason. Therefore, it becomes part of your job description to be a good listener by hearing the athletes out, even if you don't agree with them or even share their perspective.

Part 2

Interpersonal Communications

Active Listening

Part of the communication process involves being a listener. This doesn't mean passively sitting there and just partially hearing what someone is discussing. Be it a problem or another situation, you need to actively listen. Put aside everything else you're doing - that lets the individual know you're sincerely interested. Make them feel there's nobody more important than them at that moment and you're building respect and loyalty.

Fostering Trust

Having an attitude that encourages open communication and fosters trust is incredibly important for your team - even if you would rather not have to deal with athlete's personal issues or answer parents' questions. When there's a solid relationship between athletes and the coach, teams tend to win.

This is why coaches have to work toward creating an environment that welcomes real, meaningful and frequent two-way communication. Remember that one of the unwritten rules for being a coach is having contact with your athletes in a wide range of capacities on the field and off.

POINTERS ➔

In order to listen more effectively:

1 Make sure you're hearing the information correctly.

2 Encourage (and praise) to build openness.

3 Separate message content from feelings.

4 Ask appropriate questions.

5 Hear out the entire message before commenting.

6 Develop a caring attitude.

Offering Advice

An important thing to remember when an athlete has chosen to confide in you: be very careful about offering advice. While he/she may have come to you for help or advice, you might not be qualified to offer it in a given situation. Remember you're his/her coach, not a trained therapist. Have the name and number of individuals at hand who can offer legitimate help to the person, be it the school counselor or another professional.

Part 2

Interpersonal Communications

STEP BY STEP

How to Be an Active Listener

1 Cultivate an inner attitude that listening matters.

2 Think about what's being said.

3 Don't reach conclusions until the other person is through speaking.

4 Blot out distractions.

5 Concentrate on what the speaker is saying.

6 Look him/her straight in the eye.

7 Never interrupt with other business.

8 Ask occasional, appropriate questions.

9 Don't interrupt.

10 Afterward, make notes with date and time when the situation warrants it.

CHAPTER 9
AD's, SID's and Media Relations Directors

Some of the most important relationships you can build are those with your **Athletic Director, Sports Information Director,** or **Media Relations Director.** *All of these people directly affect the overall success of your team and your career, and frequently impact people's perception of you as a person and coach. Communication mishaps between coaches and AD's or SID's erode both credibility and productivity. As a result, the internal mishaps can leave coaches at a competitive disadvantage. Coaches who keep their AD's and SID's or "MRD's" informed are in a better position to receive help when they really need it. In return, a coach who is considered a good listener is more apt to be the recipient of valuable information.*

When a coach has an indifferent, strained, or hostile relationship with any of these administrators, it can create a lot more work for all of those involved. It's a no-win situation. Open communication between coaches and their AD's or SID's will ensure that there's only one winner - the team.

Athletic Directors

In the past, AD's typically rose to that post after their coaching days were over. You could count on them understanding your everyday challenges because they presumably had dealt with those challenges themselves.

No More. Contemporary AD's typically have much more diverse backgrounds. Many AD's actually earn undergraduate and/or postgraduate degrees in Sports Administration. They come from banks, legal offices, and other backgrounds, which often better equips them for the diverse and changing role of an athletic administrator.

Even if your AD was formerly a coach, he or she now faces a whole range of obligations and duties. A former coach who becomes an AD faces new challenges like financial responsibilities, personnel, public relations, media relations, and compliance "bottom lines." Their perspective has changed, and necessarily so.

So what does this mean for a coach? It means that they come to your issues with a totally different perspective, and frankly, probably don't understand sports as in the past. A winning record is no longer enough to provide you with tenure, or even a one-year contract extension. In addition to the winning in the athletic arena, you have to win at recruiting, fund raising, and a myriad of other tasks.

The AD is one of your most important constituents. Rapport, sensitivity, and persuasiveness are critical. Coaches who don't build strong, positive relationships with their AD will have a miserable existence and, in time, will probably be looking for a new job.

Have a Healthy Relationship With Your A.D.

You may think that there's no need to worry about your Athletic Director's perception of your team or yourself. His or her impressions are created through personal contact - *Right?* Not always. A coach can have a tremendous impact on the way the boss views the program.

Intentions carry a lot more weight when two people know them - so don't just suppose that the AD knows what you're thinking. Many an AD has protected a coach's job in opposition to clamoring fans because he or she knows the "real" coach, not just the one the public sees on the tube every week.

It's important to remember that it's your AD who controls the scope of your budget. When you talk with your AD, whether it's about official business or not, be mindful of his/her perception of your team and yourself and its role in the overall athletics program of your institution.

PLAY BY PLAY

How to Approach Your AD

1 Be positive.
A complainer is someone most people avoid, so
don't be one. The AD must often respond to
incessant and unnecessary complaints.

2 Be diplomatic.
Go through the proper channels when you have a
problem. In other words, don't go over the AD's
head, and don't complain to your athletes.

3 Remember that your team has needs.
In other words, remember who doles out
the dollars.

**4 Incorporate "Big Picture" visions into every
request.**
Use the following examples as your guidelines:

> *"Because we're working toward a more diverse
> student body, an increased recruiting budget
> could help us draw more..."*

> *"Beating Central University is obviously our goal.
> Accomplishing that would be easier if..."*

5 Think before you speak.
Don't approach your boss the moment an idea pops
into your head, give it time. Formulate your strategy
and then make your reasoned approach.

6 Be aware of his/her situation.
Remember, being the Athletic Director is a difficult
job. Yours isn't the only team he/she must oversee.

Part
2

Interpersonal Communications

Finding Common Ground

Under the best of circumstances, you and your AD will achieve a working relationship, which isn't just tolerable, but is a positive, mutually supportive experience. Recognize that your goals for your team are basically the same - to win with integrity and fairness. This is your common ground of understanding between you and your AD.

Setting Goals, Reaching Agreement

The very best foundation for a positive and highly productive relationship with your AD is to set mutually acceptable goals for your sports program. First, agree on the purpose, methods, and philosophy necessary to build and maintain a winning, classy program. Then, agree on the specific annual goals for three to five years ahead - such as graduation rates, win/loss records, post-season competition, student-athlete welfare, and other desired outcomes or results. Write them down and agree on them. Then, have face-to-face follow-up and feedback on the degree to which you're achieving or surpassing these goals, and refine the future ones.

This type of goal-oriented understanding promotes reasonable accountability and feedback, which are the cornerstones of a healthy working relationship between a coach and an AD. It's also the sound basis for consistent, positive communication.

Sports Information and Media Relations Directors

The relationship between a coach and the Sports Information or Media Relations Director isn't always an easy one, but it's fundamentally important to your program. Because of the typical coach's visibility within the community and often beyond, this is one professional relationship that could be as crucial to you as the one between the head coach and his or her assistants. Yet, for various reasons, it's still rarely considered truly important or cultivated to maximize its potential.

Coaches have power and visibility, but along with that comes vulnerability. A media relations person can run interference and protect you, or they can leave you largely exposed. If they are intimidated by you - if they are viewed as merely a statistician or someone who wouldn't know a strategic thought if it bit them - you won't be able to rely on them to cover your behind. On the other hand, when given a chance, the best media relations experts can help coaches develop media strategy, prepare for interviews, refine and highlight your image, and more. One of their critical roles is to help you develop promising relationships with the right people.

The SID or MRD guides the media dealings with the department, acting as a liaison between the media and the team. He or she should be plugged in to every facet of the community, campus and athletic department. The SID's job is extremely difficult because he or she is torn between loyalty to the institution and maintaining credibility with the media by remaining honest and forthright.

However, they don't work for the media - they work for you and your department. Expect a lot from them, but expect the right things. Like your best scout, the media relations person will scout out the media for you so you'll ultimately be more prepared.

In a message to the CoSIDA membership during his term as president, Baylor University's Maxey Parrish defines the contemporary SID's various jobs like this: To "write, edit, layout, design, publish, speak, produce, negotiate, organize, administer, and serve."

SID's, MRD's and the Media

Coaches tend to turn to their SID only when the headlines turn sour. It would be great if the SID could control the media, but that's impossible. Influence, yes - control, no. They can and should facilitate media relations for the team both before, and when necessary, after the interview.

Part

2

Interpersonal Communications

Building Media Muscle

SID's or MRD's can make your job easier, and you can do the same for them. They can ease media pressure and insulate you and your team from negative exposure. They also bring their gifts - candidness, intellectual skills, and talent - to the communication process. In return, you can through words and actions promote a positive attitude regarding the media with your staff and athletes.

What your athletes say to the media can be as important as what you say - their words will reflect on you and your program. Athletes can also draw positive attention to your program with very little effort. Therefore, work with your SID or MRD to provide them with the skills they need to deal with the media. Help your athletes to prepare as they would to face a formidable opponent. In actuality - they are!

Ask your SID to explain basic procedures, guidelines for interviewing, and crisis management and the media your team and/or coaching staff. He or she can address the entire group, and for the highest profile athletes, work one on one. Providing written media policies, guidelines and procedures always helps.

Increasing Media Resources

At the college level, your school may participate in the NCAA Life Skills Program. Many institutions provide media training for their athletic departments through the auspices of their Life Skills Program. The program can both facilitate and provide funding for specialized training when necessary.

POINTERS

Four Primary Sources of Media Training

1 Outside professional media trainers.

2 Working media panel discussions.

3 Your internal media relations department.

4 Professional media training products: including tapes, books, websites, etc.

At both the high school and college levels, you can use local resources such as media personalities or print reporters. There are also low-cost media training tapes that you can buy, including the audio tape series *Power Training: How to Win at the Media Game.* (Produced by *Sports Media Challenge* - see order information p. 169)

Help Your SID or MRD Develop A Successful Media Training Program for Athletes

This is something you can work with your SID or MRD on. Thorough media training for athletes, as well as staff and assistant coaches, is vital to your team's media success.

1 Have a written media policy and clear procedural guidelines to give them. Make sure they understand and follow them.

2 Help them understand the concept of "media-star vs. team exposure." This is the concept that media attention focused on one athlete isn't the same thing as media attention focused on the whole team. Give extra help to the highest profile athletes, enabling them to give strong interviews, remain humble, and be part of the team.

3 Consider the best value for your time and effort when designing a media-training program. A good compromise is to do a short, large group session to share the most needed information - then follow up with one-on-one or small groups for those with the greatest exposure. Limit most sessions to two hours, provide food as enticement, and don't schedule them late at night when concentration is most difficult.

4 Build awareness with a single media training session, but remember that the lessons are **quickly and easily forgotten**. An annual comprehensive training session followed by substantive critiques throughout the season helps athletes to better learn media skills. Condensed review/prep sessions prior to post-season play and during crises are also very beneficial.

5 Bring in an outside consultant or alumni with media experience to reinforce what you and your SID or MRP regularly tell athletes. Outsiders can reinforce your credibility and bring another healthy perspective to your audience.

6 Prioritize your information if media training is initiated by a crisis. They'll absorb only about half the information they would in normal times. Substantial critique and debriefing is imperative. Focus on their strengths, but don't avoid the weaknesses. **Note:** the best time to offer media training is in preparation for normal exposure. More information can be offered in a relaxed environment.

7 Offer all training within the framework of your home media market. In other words: have your SID or MRP explain the size market, caliber and quantity of reporters as well as any peculiarities (i.e., a Pulitzer Prize reporter who wants to win another award with your story). In addition, have them clearly indicate how your market differs from those of your competitors.

8 Use audio and videotape of mock interviews to prepare student-athletes. Like scouting and game films, people learn lots from seeing and hearing themselves on tape. Critique actual print and on-air coverage to judge the effectiveness of your preparation and to identify areas to improve.

CHAPTER 10
Recruiting

Because athletes are often the "pride and joy" of their families, you must approach them with caution. Before you walk through that door, take a moment to think about where they're coming from. Their compelling and legitimate concerns go well beyond your team and its success.

In most cases, family members want to do what is best for their child. It's likely that they have a high regard for the athlete, and his or her skill. (If you're a parent, you can probably understand that perspective.) On the other hand, some parents or guardians may be misguided, pushing the athlete way too hard. In either case, you will have a better chance of succeeding if you understand the kind of people you're dealing with.

An excited coach stands in the living room of an outstanding young athlete, enthusiastically explaining the advantages of her institution to the family. She gives them statistics on the outstanding team, shows them photographs of the state-of-the-art facility, and details the scholarship the athlete will receive. In addition, the coach tells them all about the exceptional academic standards of the school, and explains how she will personally look after the athlete and make sure that she excels both academically and on the field. She leaves the home confident that she won the family over with her persuasive sales pitch.

Two days later, the coach calls the athlete and is surprised to learn that her school isn't even in the running. She doesn't understand how her powerful and dynamic presentation could have failed to motivate the athlete and her family.

The coach didn't win the family over because she spent all of her time talking, and none of it listening. She was so busy praising the school, the team, and the facility that she forgot to ask the family what they wanted.

Successful recruiting is an information exchange, in which the family and coach share their goals and concerns for the athlete and team. Listening builds mutual respect between a coach and an athlete's family. It also helps the coach earn the family's trust, and learn about their ambitions and fears. When the focus is on their issues, instead of the virtues of the school, the family will learn all they need to know about their athlete's future at the institution.

PLAY BY PLAY

Meeting with Parents and Guardians

1 Speak to them as you would like to be spoken to.

2 Don't get upset over their lack of objectivity.

3 Make no promises prior to the meeting.

4 Avoid the phone whenever possible - the phone can give them artificial courage.

5 When appropriate and possible, meet with them in person. Offer several times to accommodate their schedule. Often, they'll give the issue more thought when they're meeting you face-to-face.

Recruiting Tips

The most difficult conversations you may have with parents is when you're sitting in their living room, trying to convince them why you're a good coach and why they should let their athlete come to your school or organization. You understand how crucial these conversations are; you've heard how coaches will try anything to win over the family. In most cases, however, what you really need are strong recruiting skills. Here are some to work on.

1 Look Your Best
Within the first four seconds you make an impression. Families want to know that you will be a good influence on their child, so look the part. Don't dress too formally, but make sure you look neat and well groomed. If you're meeting them at an event or for dinner, dress for the occasion.

2 Listen!
What are they saying they want for their child? They probably have a long list, but you need to key in to their main point. For example, if they tell you they want their son or daughter to graduate with a degree, then they must hear what you're prepared to do to help their child achieve this. Not only will listening help you earn trust, it'll give you valuable information to use when recruiting.

3 Find out - Who's the boss?
In most cases, one parent or family member is the "lead" person who will make the decisions. Watch their actions and try to decide who the lead person is, then direct more of your points to them without alienating other influencers.

4 Give them the "Home Team Advantage"
Try to make yourself comfortable in their environment. They need to know that you respect their athlete enough to get to know their family. Be careful not to point out differences in taste - that may alienate them and promote distrust. They don't want to think that their athlete will be in a totally different environment at your institution or program. If they invite you into their home, be genuine and gracious.

Part
2

Interpersonal Communications

5 Find Common Ground

When there are significant differences of opinion or problems, it's best to address them. Ignoring them typically creates barriers that are difficult to overcome. Building trust and rapport usually lays the foundation for persuasiveness.

6 Learn to Adapt

If you know the family is looking for a warm, fuzzy coach to nurture their son or daughter and that's not you, think about how you can adapt to the situation. Never lie or be something you're not. If you anticipate and are sensitive to what their hot buttons are, you'll make more progress.

CHAPTER 11
Networking

No matter how much you may want to avoid it, networking is an important part of your job. While it may often seem easier to talk to your team or co-workers, meeting new people is just as crucial to you career. The following chapter contains a few tips to keep in mind at that next event, to make your networking experience as smooth and painless as possible.

Part 2

Interpersonal Communications

PLAY BY PLAY

Overcoming Minglephobia

So, here you are at a large event. Entering the room, you realize that you don't know a soul, and every ounce of self-assurance you once possessed has disappeared. You're standing alone, frozen against the wall, in a room full of people. *What now?* Introduce yourself to the first person you come into contact with. This is an effective "ice breaker." You'll find that things become much easier from this point on.

Anxious? Welcome to the Club!
Some people deal with their fears by withdrawing; others act nervous or clumsy. It's important not to give in to your fears, especially in those first crucial moments.

Nervous? Fake it!
Relax and say to yourself, "I'm going to fake it till I make it." This simple affirmation is an effective - almost magical - way to transform terror into a positive outlook. Pretend to be happy wherever you are. Make believe that you're confident, even for ten minutes, and an amazing thing will happen - you'll actually begin to feel that way.

STEP BY STEP

Nine Steps to Working a Crowd

1 Plan For Payoffs

2 Put Others At Ease

3 Don't Get Locked In With Friends

4 Identify Common Links & Interests

5 Be Genuine

6 Listen To Ideas, Not Words

7 Limit 5 Minutes Per Person

8 Move On

9 When Appropriate Exchange Business Cards

---

1 Plan For Payoffs
Set objectives in advance that you want to achieve at the event - both personal and professional.

Personal: Meet new people with different interests.

Professional: Use this chance to promote a new, improved image to those around you.

2 Put Others At Ease
Adopt a host, not guest, mentality. Actively put others at ease. You don't have time to worry about your own discomfort. To start a conversation and be included in a group, have the host

introduce you when possible. On your own? Move to the out-side of the ring of people. Make eye contact and listen first. Wait for an opening to speak.

3 Don't Get Locked In With Friends
You already know your friends. Though it's more comfortable to talk to them, you're there to meet new people. You may never have another chance to meet today's strangers. Remember, new people expand your horizons and may be good contacts!

4 Identify Common Links and Interests
Discuss your chosen topic of interest. (Something other than the sports that you deal with every day.) Ask them about their inter-ests! Building rapport and exchanging ideas and perspectives on current events etc., helps to break boredom and adds to your enjoyment.

5 Be Genuine
Eye contact, a smile and handshake make it easier for one "real" person to connect with another. Share yourself without giving it all away. Appropriate eye contact and gestures vary dramatical-ly from one culture to another. In North America, power and interest is often conveyed with direct, sustained eye contact of 3 to 5 seconds. In the United States, a firm handshake with both men and women is appropriate.

6 Listen To Ideas, Not Words
If you're the "celebrity" guest, people will want to discover you as a person. Divide your speaking and listening time accordingly. To improve your listening skills:

> 1) Assume there's value in what a person has to say and
> 2) Search for one piece of information you can use later.

7 Limit 5 Minutes Per Person
Gauge your time to allow for meeting several groups of people. Have a short, two-way conversation with four or five people within a half-hour. Comment on the unusual or interesting. This makes short conversations more fulfilling, and quick exits become less troublesome.

Part
2

Interpersonal Communications

8 Move On

Your responsibility is to the entire group, not one or two individuals. Be gracious but firm. Have a special closing comment so you won't wonder how to politely say good-bye, like: "See you at the next event." You can introduce or include someone on the edge of the group to the others who are there, then quietly leave.

9 When Appropriate, Exchange Business Cards

Keep yours in your right pocket (if you are right handed), and put those you collect in your left pocket. Write a descriptive note on the back of the cards you collect to help you remember the face that goes with the card.

How Not to Work a Room

While it's important to focus on the positive aspects of mingling, it's also necessary to be aware of the negatives so that you can avoid them. The following are some pointers that will help you avoid any mingling pitfalls.

Here's What *Not* To Do:

1 Complain about your boss, staff, or team.

2 Gossip about colleagues or others in the room.

3 Discuss salaries, contracts, etc.

4 Hide in the corner - alone or with people you already know.

5 Talk about scandals or crisis that reflect poorly on others at the event.

6 Drink too much.

7 Use one of the following *conversation killers:*

> *"Don't be ridiculous!"*
>
> *"I know exactly what you're thinking!"*
>
> *"That will never work…"*
>
> *"Are you crazy?"*
>
> *"When I was your age, I always…"*
>
> *"Everybody should…"*
>
> *"That's the way we have always done it…"*

Part

2

Interpersonal Communications

WORKSHEET

Speaking Worksheet - Content

Develop Your One-on-One Speaking Content

When you speak to people one-on-one, it's important to be aware of how you sound. You want your ideas to sound intelligent and well thought out so that people will want to listen to you. Therefore, you should constantly be on the lookout for good content. If you present yourself as an informed, well-spoken person, your ideas will be received enthusiastically.

Test your content by answering the following questions. Your goal is to answer "yes" to all three yes-or-no questions. After answering them, use the worksheet included to help develop your speaking content.

What is my most important, number one message?

_____

_____

_____

When I spoke in conversation today...

*I determined my most important
message and articulated it.*   Yes   No

I articulated the idea in one sentence.   Yes   No

*I repeated my main idea for added
emphasis at appropriate times.*   Yes   No

WORKSHEET

Speaking Worksheet - Content con't

Build Content Every Day
Newspapers Read Today:

❏ *USA Today*   ❏ *Local Newspaper*
❏ *Wall Street Journal*   ❏ *Other*

Magazines/Books Begun or Continued:

_____
_____

What article/topic did I use in conversation?

_____
_____

What article/topic was I most interested in?

_____
_____

Who did I talk about the article/topic with?

_____
_____

*I added the following new word to my
useable vocabulary today:*

_____

How did I use it?

_____
_____

Part 3

Building Your Image

When I was coaching, the one thought that I would try to get across to my players was that everything I do each day, everything I say, I must first think what effect it will have on everyone involved.

Frank Layden
Former Head Coach, Utah Jazz
NBA & Sporting News
Coach of the Year 1983, 1984

CHAPTER 12
How's Your Image?

Most people want to develop and communicate a positive image. You can do that by keeping your image in mind with every interaction you have. Spreading a positive image is also a way to ward off negative media attention. If you and your athletes project a positive message to the community, that's how the media will portray you. The goal, of course is - *If your team is being covered, make it good news.* Even if you're hit with bad press, you've the ability to turn it around by focusing the media on the positive stories in your program.

Enhance Your Coaching Magnetism

"Coaching Magnetism" isn't a PR term some executive invented; it's something you'll find in the best coaches. These are the ones with the ability to attract the best athletes and supporters to them. Often you find that athletes retire, transfer, or are traded when a favorite coach leaves a team. For example, when former Boston College basketball coach Jim O'Brien moved to Ohio State University, some of his star players followed him to Ohio. Athletes regularly choose to compete or not to compete for organizations based on the coach.

Magnetic Coaches...

Inspire. Bring a positive and dynamic perspective to all situation.

Influence. Understand that athletes look up to them and follow their lead.

Set Expectations. They know what they want and state their messages clearly.

Persuade. They win people over to their way of thinking.

Cheerlead. They bolster self-esteem and confidence.

...Are in Demand!

Part
3

Building Your Image

PLAY BY PLAY

Personal Magnetism

Try these techniques to improve your Coaching Magnetism.

Inspirational Coaches...

Make an appeal to strong values.
"Being the best" or "outperforming the competition" are strong trigger points.

Ask the right questions.
It's often better to ask a question than to tell people what you want them to do. For example, a coach might ask a question like: How many of you want to win? This elicits emotion and inspires them to try harder.

Appeal to multiple senses.
You want athletes to hear and feel your message. This will help them to imagine the total experience of winning.

Inspire people with success stories.
These stories are a great way to inspire others, and they encourage others to improve themselves. However, don't over-use them, because you don't want to appear to be living in the past.

[Adapted from Andrew J. DuBrin's *Personal Magnetism* [2]]

CHAPTER 13
Representing Your Team

As a Coach, *you're aware of the role athletes play in representing the team to the community. But do you think about your own role? Obviously, when you're asked to speak at the local Rotary, you wouldn't want to show up smelling of liquor. You, like most coaches, know how to conduct yourself at these events.*

It's just like you tell your athletes: **when you're out in public you're not only representing yourself, you're representing your school, institution and/or team.** As you've no doubt learned, this applies to you too. But public events aren't the only interactions where you have to be mindful of your actions - critical contact happens in your everyday life. Each time you speak to a supporter, alumni member or even your mailman, you're representing yourself as well as your team and institution.

Be Aware of Your Role as Representative

Everything you do or say reflects on your program. What is it that you want people to know or feel about the team that you coach? Yes, much of this is common sense, but it's forgotten quite often. Even if you consider yourself to be a behind-the-scenes character, you're regarded as a public figure and must be mindful of the responsibility you have to your school, team and program.

When you're faced with questions such as "What is wrong with Student X?" you must be careful. Don't critique individual athletes in front of a group such as fans or alumni - it can be humiliating for the athlete and it makes your team look bad. There's a delicate balance between confidence and criticism, so while it's OK to praise standouts, avoid extreme praise as well as criticism. If you don't, you may threaten the chemistry of your team by pitting athletes against one another.

Part
3

Building Your Image

PLAY BY PLAY

Be Confident With Fan Groups and Alumni

Their support of you and your program is critical to its survival and success. Alumni want to know that to you, they're more than financial supporters of the athletic program. Believe it or not, to most alumni, you're a celebrity. They simply want to be a part of what you're doing.

Try speaking to support groups and alumni without asking for anything.
Let them take the lead. This will make interaction more comfortable and take some pressure off you.

Remember that most people are supporters of the entire athletic program.
Let them know that you are too. Discuss, in a supportive manner, an event or coach in another sport.

Project some interest in their non-sports related business.
Do you share common hobbies? Have you traveled to any of the same cities or countries?

Avoid political or controversial topics.
These might alienate prospective allies. If they arise - change the subject or expect to deal with the ramifications.

Share your values and life goals.
Sharing these adds to the positive perception others have of you, especially if they're considered to be positive and worthy goals.

CHAPTER 14
Visibility: High Risk/High Reward

Because of their highly visible position, coaches live in fish-bowls. This creates a situation that can result in both opportunities and problems. It's therefore important to be aware of your visibility so that you're prepared for both positive and negative attention.

The kind of attention a coach receives can be attributed to the popularity or success of the team, the current climate of sports, or a preexisting public image. The best tool you can use to regulate the nature of the attention you receive is to be in control of your behavior. Your behavior is what people use to determine your image.

Mention the name Woody Hayes or Bobby Knight and you immediately picture their sideline behavior almost as much as their athletic achievements. The "Woody Hayes Outburst" was so well known that it became synonymous with Ohio State Football. Although Hayes had the best record in OSU history, he's remembered for losing his temper after the Buckeyes fumbled in a bowl game and striking a Clemson player. Bobby Knight's outbursts are often on the national news and have made their way to parodies on Saturday Night Live. Although some accept it as part of his personality, Knight's reputation as a coach will never outlive the perception some people have of him.

People watch you when you're on the sidelines during any competition. Whether you like it or not, that means that's how most people judge you. When you're on the sidelines, you're also going through the most stressful part of your job. You have to learn to balance your coaching style, and be aware of the danger of destroying your reputation with your behavior - on the sidelines, or anywhere else.

Part
3

Building Your Image

How Not to be Remembered for Your Antics

Whether you walk, stalk, jump, scream, prance or dance along the sidelines you must be mindful of your conduct. It probably seems like the last thing you've time to think about, but take a moment to consider how you look to others. You can express yourself in many ways without looking like a lunatic.

It's said that George Seifert, the former coach of Super Bowl champions the San Francisco 49ers, disciplined his players with a look. They could identify it and knew it was for them. Rick Pitino, during time outs, often jumps from his seat aggressively clapping and smiling at his approaching players. What most fans and television viewers don't know is he's sometimes chastising his players in vivid language. Aware of the importance of his image, Pitino is said to have developed this style out of necessity and because he obviously found it to be effective.

POINTERS ➔

Sideline Guidelines

There's no one correct philosophy to sideline conduct, but try following some of the guidelines:

Record yourself - view the tape as if you're a stranger watching. What impression do you make? Better yet, ask a family member or friend how you look.

Think about what kind of coach you want to be and translate that through your actions. Do you want to be known as the coach who stays cool under pressure? If you do, then be aware of your aggressive body language.

Always remember that people are watching you. Supporters, parents, and future employers are watching and listening. You don't want them to decide that they don't like what they see.

CHAPTER 15
The Final Score in Perspective

It makes no difference *whether you're pulling ice cubes from your collar and hoping that Gatorade doesn't stain or you're wiping tears as you toss your playsheets, you must have a plan for addressing your team after it's all over.*

Win or lose, the approach is very similar. You must learn to control your team's emotions, both high and low, to avoid the pitfalls that result from going too far in either direction.

All Eyes on You

Your athletes will look for your response after an event. If you find yourself unable to control your own emotions, how can you expect athletes who may think they have more at stake to be in command of theirs?

If, after the big win, you're too busy leading supporters in a rousing rendition of "We are the Champions" to talk with your team, you're sending a clear message to them it's time to let loose. On the other hand, if you stalk off the field without addressing your team after a loss, you're signaling to your athletes that anger and rage are acceptable reactions.

How to Keep it in Perspective

Before the Event:
You can't predict if you'll win or lose, but you can be ready for either outcome. Prepare the focus of your post-event talk before it even begins. Ask yourself:

> *What will you say, win or lose?*

> *What feeling do you want to leave the team and others with?*

You may also want to think of advice or catch phrases to leave your athletes with. You can talk to them through the media, and ultimately, you can communicate with the media and public through your athletes.

After the Event:
Win or lose, it's important to address your athletes as soon after the event as possible. Avoid the temptation to hide after a loss or spend too much time relishing a victory.

Call the whole team together for this address. You'll send a message that the team is most important, victory or defeat. Don't allow athletes to be late or miss a meeting. If anyone leaves early, they can't discuss the positives and negatives of the event while it's still fresh in their minds.

After a Win

1 *Keep your composure* - If you fear not having your emotions in check before addressing the team, take a few minutes to relax. The following is one technique that has proven successful.

Find a place to sit in relative solitude, sit upright focusing your attention on a spot on the floor between your feet with your chin resting on your chest, and breathe. Breathe deeply, using this time to prepare your comments. Eliminate all unnecessary thoughts by allowing yourself to fully examine the focus of your impending address. Breathing deeply releases natural hormones (endorphines) throughout your body that relieve stress.

2 *Keep things in perspective* - Don't over-celebrate. Remember that your athletes will soon leave your sight. The message you send after a big win needs to be the right message. Don't give your athletes permission to over-celebrate with your actions.

3 *Focus on the team's victory* - It's fine to highlight the performance of individual competitors, but don't allow the team to lose sight of itself and every member's contribution.

4 *Allow athletes to contribute only after you've spoken* - Having set the tone with your words, you should feel confident that an athlete's post-event remarks will support and strengthen your message.

POINTERS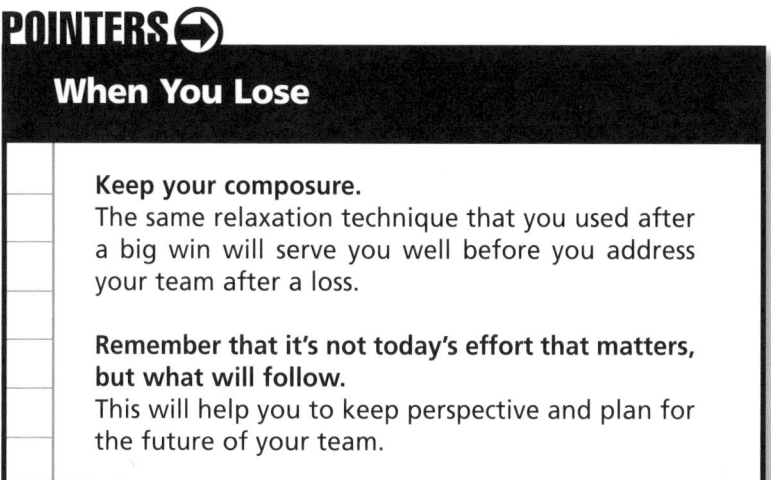

When You Lose

Keep your composure.
The same relaxation technique that you used after a big win will serve you well before you address your team after a loss.

Remember that it's not today's effort that matters, but what will follow.
This will help you to keep perspective and plan for the future of your team.

With this said, remember: You Won! Let the athletes know that you're aware of their success and appreciate their enthusiasm, while emphasizing the importance of moderation in celebration.

Choose Your Words Carefully

1 Avoid Negativity
No matter how angry or frustrated you may feel, avoid individual criticism, even of yourself at this time. Try to keep everything group oriented. Using sarcasm or ridicule can also be dangerous, because what you may think is funny or poignant at the moment may come back to haunt you later. Finally, don't talk down to the athletes. They know how, and probably why, they lost.

Be mindful of the fact that whatever you say is going to be criticism to some extent, but it should turn them on, not off. And there's most likely a better opportunity to point out strengths and weaknesses and use them as a teaching tool later.

Part
3

Building Your Image

How Not to be Negative

Counterproductive:	Alternative:
"We/I failed to..."	"Here's what I/we learned..."
"Always," "Never,"	"Sometimes,"
"Everything," "Nothing,"	"Often," etc.
"We are in trouble."	"We will bounce back."
"We'll try..."	"We will..."
"We haven't/didn't..."	"We can..."

2 **Forget About Yourself for Awhile**
Defeats are difficult, but remember the team did the actual losing, and they feel bad enough without the added responsibility of having let you down.

3 **Begin and End Your Remarks with a Note of Genuine Praise Whenever Possible**
No matter how badly you feel, or devastating the loss, highlight their effort, teamwork, desire, or some other positive when it exists.

By keeping these suggestions in mind, you'll become a better communicator and a better coach. Everyone knows the challenge of being a good loser or a humble victor, but the responsibility for making these things possible falls to you.

CHAPTER 16
Accepting Awards Like A Star

Hopefully, some time in your coaching career you will get the chance to walk on stage and accept an award. When you do finally get on that stage, you don't want to look like a fool and mumble a few easily forgotten words.

The award might be for something relatively small, like being recognized by your school for the good season everyone expected, or for your longevity. Or, you may be recognized for something highly publicized such as being named conference, state, or national coach of the year.

No matter how minor or major the event, when it's you, one of your athletes, or your team's time in the spotlight, remember to do the following:

**1 Express Your Respect for the Organization
Presenting the Award**
This could mean learning something about the organization or how you were selected before the night of the presentation. Find out if there was a voting committee, a chairperson, nominations, etc. and focus your appreciation accordingly.

2 Share the Credit
It isn't just your coaching skills that got you the award - other people contributed as well. Take this time to express appreciation to your Athletic Director, owner, staff, or athletes. And don't forget your family! Whether you believe it or not, the support of all these people is important.

Receiving awards is an exciting and rewarding experience. However, it can be nerve-racking if you're unprepared. Make sure that your audience, even if they forget the award, doesn't forget you. Enjoy the spotlight!

Part 3

Building Your Image

PLAY BY PLAY

Things to Remember When Accepting

Thank your team members, other coaches and family members for their support and enthusiasm. Make sure your sincerity is obvious.

Where appropriate, pay respects to a friend whose name will mean something to the audience. Don't repeat a laundry list of everyone you've ever known, this will bore the audience.

Be humble but not shy! There's no substitute for the power of humility in the spotlight. By the same token, a shy award recipient seems to lack the confidence that was probably necessary to deserve the award in the first place.

Pass the buck and praise the competition, but only if you really mean it.

Give people a glimpse of the "real you." Tell a story no one in the audience knows.

An appropriate touch of humor always adds to the occasion, but don't tell old jokes. Again, knowing your audience will help you to gauge their response.

Make your speech a conversation with the audience. This doesn't mean engaging them in a dialogue. Their reactions to your words are enough.

When you've said it all, sit down.

WORKSHEET

Image Worksheet

Choose three words that most people in the following categories would use to describe you.

Public   1 _____
            2 _____
            3 _____

Athletes/Coaches
            1 _____
            2 _____
            3 _____

Media   1 _____
            2 _____
            3 _____

What have you done to create that image?
Intentionally   Unintentionally

_____
_____
_____
_____

How do these perceptions differ from the real you?

_____
_____
_____
_____
_____

Part **3**

Building Your Image

WORKSHEET

Image Worksheet con't.

Target Image
Choose the 3 words that you <u>want people to use</u> to describe you.

Public   **1** _____
         2 _____
         3 _____

Athletes/Coaches
         1 _____
         2 _____
         3 _____

Media   **1** _____
         2 _____
         3 _____

What outside factors would get in the way of you building that image?

_____
_____
_____

What outside factors can help foster that image?

_____
_____
_____

WORKSHEET

Image Worksheet con't.

What internal factors - such as reticence, fear, anxiety, or aggression - would get in the way of building that image?

_____

_____

_____

What internal factors - such as confidence, faith, or gritty determination - would help foster that image?

_____

_____

_____

How close are you to achieving this image, 1-10?

[worst] **1 2 3 4 5 6 7 8 9 10** [best]

Identify three things that you will consciously do to help create or enhance your image.

1 _____

2 _____

3 _____

Part
3

Building Your Image

Part 4

The Media: Friend or Foe?

My ability is to digest a lot of
information which I dispense
calmly and articulately while
everyone around me
is going bananas.

Bryant Gumbel
Broadcast Journalist

CHAPTER 17
Your Media Game Plan

Today, *public scrutiny of coaches and athletes can be harsh and unrelenting. Being the coach is difficult enough. Added to that, sports stories are no longer found just on the sports page or aired on Sunday sports TV programs. Good and bad stories make the headlines on the front page of the newspaper, lead television newscasts, and now the Internet. This high visibility makes coaching one of the hardest jobs in the athletic world today. The spotlight creates an uncomfortable focus on your decisions and how they're made.*

Sports Is News - Performing in the Spotlight

The media will shine the spotlight on your program for many reasons. If a scandal rocks your program, expect every misstep in bold headlines. If there's unexpected success, count on a deluge of attention for the winning team. Whatever the case, here's what to keep in mind regarding the media.

1 *How Much Coverage Are You Receiving?*
No one can predict how much media attention a program will receive but you must at least think about the possibilities. Before the media calls, think about the **volume, frequency,** and **type of coverage** your team could receive and how ready you are for it.

2 *Polish Your Interviewing Skills*
Know how to deliver a great interview and make positive contributions to an outstanding story.

3 *Provide Media Tools For Others*
Give others, including athletes, the tools to effectively represent your program through the media. Don't send them out to compete in the arena of public exposure without the best equipment and training available. You wouldn't send them out to an athletic contest without the proper preparation and equipment.

Part
4

The Media: Friend or Foe?

PLAY BY PLAY

Pre-Game Prep - Before the Interview

As soon as a reporter calls you for an interview, take control of the situation. Here are questions you, your Media Relations Director, or your Sports Information Director should ask in advance so you can be better prepared and decide if the interview is worth your time and effort.

1 What is the focus of the story?
Most reporters know before they leave the newsroom what focus they're after.

2 Who else is being interviewed for this story?
If the reporter lists your enemies, this is a good time to suggest other people to contact who will reinforce or enhance your perspective. At least, you can anticipate what they'll say to prepare your comments.

3 What's their deadline?
Expect a more in-depth and lengthy interview if the reporter has days rather than hours, or even minutes, to put a story together.

4 Taped or live?
For television and radio interviews, it's important to ask if you're going to be taped. Ask if sections will be used later and edited for sound bites, or if this is a live interview which means the interview is broadcast as it happens. If live- will it have call-ins or audience participation of any kind?

Game Time

Once you know where the reporter is coming from, you can *plan the one message you want to get across* during the interview. Whether you're facing good or bad media inquiries, you decide what you want to communicate. Interviews can always be a positive source of public relations, enhancing the neutral or positive messages and neutralizing the negative ones. Here are four ways to win!

Four Ways to Win

1 Listen to the Question
This may sound easy, but if you're distracted even for a second you can miss the question and end up giving an inappropriate answer. You can also be stumped by emotional words or phrases within the question if you answer without hearing or understanding the whole thing. Ask yourself... *What is he or she trying to get at?* Instead of listening to the words spoken, listen to the meaning behind them. That gives you greater latitude to answer the question.

2 Clarify
It's okay to ask a reporter to repeat the question or even rephrase it. Don't be reluctant or too shy to ask for this. Often they'll ask questions that don't make sense. Asking questions of the reporter helps balance the power between the interviewer and you.

3 Be Direct
On controversial matter, make your point in 20 seconds or less. Expanding beyond the original question can cause problems later. If your answers are too long, the reporter will edit or paraphrase, and that's when they'll probably lose some of your meaning. Speak in complete sentences to avoid being taken out of context.

4 Avoid Jargon
Be precise and speak in terms the public can understand. Not everyone will understand your professional language. Help others understand by painting pictures with your words.

Part
4

The Media: Friend or Foe?

Student Confidentiality

When you speak to the media about your team or athletes, there's another issue that you must take into consideration. Student Confidentiality is protected by law, and should be protected by your athletic department as well.

The **Buckley Amendment,** also known as the **Student Privacy Act,** dictates what information a coach can release about a student-athlete. The practical application of the Amendment has to do with grade point averages. Under no circumstances can an athletic department release the GPA of a student to the press or anyone else. If the student is over 18, even the parents cannot receive the information unless it comes from the student.

Student-athletes can sometimes sign a waiver to release that information, but unless there's authorization, their grades are protected. In other words, coaches can be (and have been) fired for releasing a student-athlete's grades to the public.

Athletic departments are often allowed access to student-athlete grades, but only for the purpose of assigning tutors. This information cannot be used in any other way.

CHAPTER 18
Winning at the Media Game

When the media turns its spotlight on you, you may ask yourself "Why Me?" The reporter's calls may come at the worst time, when the team is facing a crisis or intense pressure. While you may dread them, media interviews are a great source of publicity. Follow these guidelines and you'll learn how to deal with the scrutiny and boost your public image.

Interviewers aren't all Ted Koppel or Dan Rather

Don't assume that the interviewer has researched you or your program. Many times, all they've been assigned to do is show up. Take time to review the basics in this chapter before you launch into your game plan.

Interview Guidelines

1 Use the Quick Bleed. Interviews can be a great source of public relations, attracting more fans and building support for you and your team. But what happens if the focus is negative? Typically, the best approach is to "go for the quick bleed, not a slow hemorrhage." Put negatives behind you as quickly as possible. Avoid using and repeating negative words or phrases.

> *"We're hearing rumors about three athletes being investigated on grand theft charges. Are they true?"*

> *"There's absolutely **no** truth to that rumor."*

Repeating the word "rumor" reinforces the negative connotation of the word. Instead, try the following response:

> *"Guys, you know that I don't comment on unsubstantiated claims."*

2 Honesty is the best policy. When you're wrong, admit it. This increases your credibility with reporters and the public. Admitting, instead of denying a mistake, puts you on a human level.

3 Avoid appearing defensive. Try to be as insightful as possible. You don't want to appear to be hiding anything.

4 Remember that interviews are a good thing. Use interviews to promote yourself and your agenda. Use the interview to gain new and increased support for you and your team.

5 Promote Your Agenda. One way to enhance your performance is to decide what you want to communicate in advance and then do it. This is true whether you're facing good or bad media inquiries.

Anticipate what reporters want, then answer their questions with your agenda in mind. Don't be led by reporters' questions. Going into a media situation with your own agenda can help form the direction and tone of the story. Effectively, you're balancing the power!

POINTERS ➡

A Few Broadcast Tips

Speak in your normal tone of voice. The taped interview is like a conversation; you don't need to over-project your voice as if you're addressing a packed stadium, just speak as you normally do in conversation.

Made a mistake? Start over. As long as the interview is taped, not live (which means it's broadcast as you speak), you can correct mistakes. If you don't like your answer simply say, "I'm sorry," and begin your answer again.

Unless you have some broadcast experience, don't worry about looking at the camera. Simply give your answer to the person asking the questions. The camera will find you, just concentrate on getting your message out.

CHAPTER 19
Where Will You Have to Perform?

There are a variety of mediums in which you'll have to perform - the media isn't limited to newspaper sports pages and ESPN. Your team could be featured in a news program or magazine feature; or you might be asked to participate in an online chat session with fans. In any case, the more prepared you are for these types of media coverage, the better.

Television - News Programs, Talk Shows, Magazines

In addition to the interview guidelines in this chapter, there are a few things to keep in mind about television. It's a visual medium, so *how you look is as important as what you say.* The people interviewing you don't care how you look, so you have to. This includes your overall appearance, how you're dressed, how you conduct yourself, your facial expressions, and your body language.

How to Outsmart the Camera

1 Appearance: Without makeup, you may look pale. Be clean-cut and well groomed (guys - beware the 5 o'clock shadow). If you tend to have a sweaty forehead, use *clear antiperspirant* on it. Nobody has to know it's there but you!

When you select your clothes, avoid small prints and patterns, they look busy on the screen. Also, avoid white because most cameras still don't handle white well.

2 Camera Angles: Don't be caught off-guard by the camera. You can be aware of where it is without being self-conscious about it. Try to position yourself at a flattering angle. At least two-thirds of your face should be facing the camera.

3 Body Language: Use gestures, just as you would before a large audience, but make them smaller. Large gestures will overwhelm on the small screen and you could be left with arms but no

Part 4

The Media: Friend or Foe?

hands on TV. Be more animated than when you're in person because TV tends to make you two-dimensional. In other words - **project energy.**

Print Journalism - Features, Columns, and News Stories

Written articles may seem like less of a concern to you, because you don't have to be videotaped or interviewed live. However, print journalism carries its own challenges. Most interviews are audiotaped, and the reporter generally has more time to process the information.

POINTERS ➔
Keep the Following Facts in Mind When Preparing for a Print Story:

1 Interviews generally last longer.

2 Stories can be read and reread.

3 The stories are longer and contain more substance.

4 More people can and probably will be interviewed.

5 Reporters have an angle that they'll build their story around if you don't intentionally guide them.

Remember that print and broadcast reporters are trained observers. They'll build the story around several things, including your perceived attitude, then they look for indicators to expand these perceptions and add texture. In other words, if a reporter wants to portray you as a hothead, he or she will look for characteristics to put in the story, such as: "The coach appeared agitated, and it was obvious that the crisis was getting to him." It could have been your tone of voice, stony stare, or reputation that gave the reporter that idea.

They'll edit what you say for length and content, as well as shock value, so make sure that your comments are short and to the point. As in any forum, remember: don't say anything that could easily be misconstrued or misquoted. Always speak in complete sentences, not fragments, if you want them to keep your thoughts intact. (Refer to the chapter *Avoiding Misquotes... and Being Taken Out of Context* p. 133 for more on this.)

Radio Talk Shows

Radio talk shows are a part of today's media. It's difficult to avoid this growing phenomenon if you want to promote your team. If you look at these shows as an opportunity, and know how to avoid the pitfalls, you can use the forum to your advantage.

One benefit of radio talk shows is that they're timely and in depth. Timeliness is important; especially when there's a crisis or issue that's causing trouble for your team. You can explain your team's side of things, just make sure you know what points you'll make and what issues you'll address before you go on. You can refer to these issues when other, more controversial topics are brought up.

One drawback, however, is that these shows often aren't well informed or balanced. The host will often bring on a coach or expert in order to discuss a specific issue - find out what it is in advance. Typically, issues are brought up to spur debate or conflict. Don't allow yourself to fall into this trap - stay cool and collected, and stick to your original points.

Part

4

The Media: Friend or Foe?

Find out in advance whether or not you'll be on a call-in show. These shows can be a challenge because you don't know whom you'll be talking to. You may have to respond to difficult questions and misinformation. Those who call in rarely have inside information and usually are glad to speculate based on minimal or no facts at all. Many callers simply like to hear themselves talk. However, don't patronize callers, it will alienate other more informed or moderate listeners.

POINTERS ⊖

When Preparing For Call-in Shows, Remember:

1 Your audience on these shows will be mostly hard core sports fans, if not your fans.

2 Questioners may have little or no knowledge of what they're asking about.

3 Anybody can call in - so you may have to respond to rumors, opinions, or speculation.

4 The temperament of these callers can range from adoring to hostile.

Internet Chat Sessions

While you may never have considered participating in an online chat session, they often make sense and are a wonderful medium to talk to fans that you can't normally reach. You may consider doing it yourself, or having an athlete or assistant coach participate. The Internet is a new medium, and it has wide-open possibilities - make the most of it! (See the chapter *Plug Your Team Into the Internet*, p. 135)

Keep in mind, however, that information on the Internet moves very quickly, and you must be brief. Therefore, don't try to address large issues or problems in this format. (Refer to the section "Using the Net to Set the Record Straight," p. 152, in the chapter *Crisis and the Media*.)

CHAPTER 20
How to Get Coverage

There may be one team in your region or league that's always getting positive media attention. It could be that they're the team with the best record and the ones sure to win. It also could be that they take a media-friendly approach and understand how to win the media game. Here are some ideas to get your team covered.

At the high school level or at other institutions, it may be part of the coach's job - however, at many institutions it's the Sports Information Director, Media Relations Director, or a PR professional who will take the responsibility. If you know of a good story within your team, help these people out by bringing it to their attention so they can draw interest and attention.

While sports departments are passionate about covering sports, time and resources limit them. The easier you can make it on them, the more coverage you'll get.

Part
4

The Media: Friend or Foe?

STEP BY STEP

Increase Your Coverage

1 Check Your Local Listings
Watch the local sports coverage in your area. Which stations offer special sports shows? Call in to the sports department and find out who's in charge of putting together those shows. Once you have them on the phone...

2 Invite Them to an Event or Practice
Most media outlets don't cover something simply because they're not aware of when or where the competition is going on, or the implications.

3 Offer Them Video Footage
Many stations don't have the staff to cover every event. Offer to provide them with videotape. Timing is the key. They won't run something a day old. You need to get the tape to the station, in a professional format they can use, in time for that night's newscast.

4 Call in Your Scores
Again, if the station or paper doesn't have the information, they can't run it. Even having someone call in your final score can get you on the air and in print. They'll love it even more if you can include the names of athletes who made key plays or turned in outstanding performances.

CHAPTER 21
Tackling the Tough Questions

In any interview, you may be asked difficult or leading questions. You must be prepared for the questions in order to answer them correctly and carefully. By anticipating what kinds of questions you will be asked, you can formulate your answer so that it reflects the best interests of you and your team.

"Off-The-Record" Questions

> *"Between you and me, and this is off-the-record, isn't there a lot more involved here?"*

Never preface a bit of information with "this is off the record" unless you want it attributed to you. There's no such thing as "off-the-record." Don't answer.

Hypothetical Questions

> *"If your defense doesn't develop as quickly as you expect... then what?"*

Don't answer hypotheticals. Restate the question you think they want answered. If you're comfortable, then give a positive response specific to the general issue.

> *"Our athletes are committed to improving our defense week by week."*

Yes-or-No Questions

> *"Do you think the referee's call was fair - yes or no?*

Few things are ever as simple as "yes" or "no," "black" or "white." If the issue has a gray area, point it out and explain why you're giving your answer.

> *"Although the call hurt us, I think officials make calls as they see them."*

Part
4

The Media: Friend or Foe?

"What Do You Think Mr. X Thinks?" Questions

> *"In preparing for next week's match-up, what do you think Coach X will do to prepare his team?"*

Don't ever presume to know what someone else thinks. Speak for yourself.

Ranking Questions

> *"Name your team's two biggest assets."*

Don't be forced into listing only two issues if there are more. You risk leaving another important one out because you're answering the question literally. If you do respond, try a different approach.

> *"I think our biggest assets are raw talent, attitude, and willingness to work hard to improve ever week."*

Non-Question Questions

> *"Your team has received a lot of publicity lately."*

Either ask what the questioner means specifically - then respond or make a verbal transition to whatever you want to talk about.

The "A or B?" Questions

> *"What's more important to you - talent or preparation?"*

Don't be cornered into an inappropriate choice. An appropriate answer might be:

> *"I think that it's important for every coach to prepare the talent he has on the team. You can't separate one from the other."*

The "WHY" Questions

*"Most people in your position would say that.
Why should we believe you?"*

Fall back on your strengths. Speak only in a positive manner, never state the negative. It gives credence through repetition.

False Premise Questions

"Now that you've proven yourself to be totally insensitive to the issue, how can you turn it around?"

Correct the misconception or misstatement first, then go on to deal with the facts.

Open Questions:

"So tell me more details about your game plan."

This is your opportunity to set the agenda. You can make the most of this time by setting your communication objective in advance. If you do this, you will know your precise direction and destination.

In addition to these seemingly hostile questions, you'll also have to be prepared for the flip side. You may have to answer questions that don't seem well planned out at all. Remember though, like the tough questions above, your attitude and reaction to these questions is vital. So when you prepare, think tough, but also be ready for questions that are like the examples on the following page.

Part

4

The Media: Friend or Foe?

Typical or Obvious Questions

"So, do you feel good about today's win?"

Challenge yourself to try and answer in an unexpected way. Take the opportunity to position yourself and the team. Push your agenda!

"If you don't take time to enjoy a win, then there's no fun in playing."

Repetitive Questions

"Is this a playoff team?"

Not only will you be asked this several times during a winning season, but also it's basically an "unanswerable" question. "Yes" is too cocky. "No" isn't confident.

A possible answer to this question is:

"If we can respond positively to the challenges we face for the rest of the season, then I think we have a chance to be a playoff team."

Questions that Seem Dumb or Uninformed

"Is it important that the team learn to shoot better in order to be more competitive?"

In this situation, try to avoid mocking the questioner. Often, a dash of humor will come in handy:

"Well, if we want to score more than the opponent, then it's important..."

Inappropriate Questions

"We understand that J.J. is flunking history, which would make him ineligible. Is that true?"

Remember that at the college level, you're not free to disclose confidential information regarding the grades, academic standing, or other private issues regarding a student-athlete. This information is covered under the **Buckley Amendment**, and your institution's legal department should provide you with this important information. For your own protection and that of your athletes, department, and institution, you must understand and abide by this federal law or reap the consequences.

Controversial Questions

> *"Is it true that this is a team in turmoil?"*

In this example, turmoil is too strong a word. A good response would be something like:

> *"We are rebuilding and trying to mesh the new with the old. Individuals will need to adjust for the good of the whole."*

Another good response:

> *"That is too strong a word. We are rebuilding."*

The best way to handle a controversial matter is to acknowledge the question then bridge to your agenda. Don't repeat negative phrases/words.

You need to view these questions as a good opportunity to win new fans and renew interest for loyal followers. Draw answers from your senses and personal vantage point.

No matter what kinds of questions you're asked, your ultimate job is to educate the reporter (and the audience) about your issues and your team. Stick to your agenda and goals.

Part
4

The Media: Friend or Foe?

CHAPTER 22
Avoiding Misquotes... and Being Taken Out of Context

Misquotes can be dangerous and costly to your team and orga-nization. Speaking to the media can be very rewarding if you have the tools to avoid such pitfalls as misquotes and misleading sound bites. Use these quick and easy steps to help prevent them.

1 Be Yourself
Don't stiffen up when faced with a camera or reporter. Relax and share your enjoyment in the sport. In other words, be human.

2 20 Second Rule
Make your point in 20 seconds or less. Elaborate if there's time, interest, or need.

3 Be Precise
Avoid generalities. Use specific examples that clarify and make people care about your view.

Pocket Guide to Avoiding "Misquotes"

20 Second Rule
Make your point in twenty seconds or less. Elaborate only if there is need, interest and time.

Be Precise
Avoid generalities that can be misinterpreted. Use specific examples that clarify and make the audience/readers care about your view.

Don't Be Baited
Remain composed at all cost.

Avoid Jargon
Speak in terms the general public will understand.

Live vs. Tape
Agree to a live or live-to-tape interview that will not be edited. The audience will hear your words not a paraphrased version of the real thing.

Build Rapport
For balanced coverage, set the ground work in advance. Trust and a basic understanding of your operation reduce misinterpretation.

© Communications Concepts
Charlotte, NC 704/365-5027 FAX# 704/366-9556

4 Don't Be Baited
Remain calm at all costs. Don't fly off the handle or give a knee-jerk reaction, or it'll come back to haunt you.

5 Don't Use Jargon
Use words that the general public can understand. It builds audi-ences, and that means more fans in the stands.

6 Don't Forget - You're Always On
If you can see a microphone, camera, or reporter's notebook, assume that your words and actions are being recorded.

[Based on the popular laminated reference card **"The Pocket Guide to Avoiding Misquotes"** available from **Sports Media Challenge**.]

Part
4

The Media: Friend or Foe?

CHAPTER 23
Plug Your Team into the Internet

Because it's relatively new, many professionals don't take the *Internet seriously. But fans do. Today, more than 50% of the people that access the Internet use it for sports information.*

Take a Break from Coaching and Do Some Surfing!

If you browse the World Wide Web, you will find countless sites devoted to teams, athletes, institutions, and others. You may even find a page devoted to yourself! Keep in mind, some of these sites are poorly constructed and may carry inaccurate, misleading, or simply bizarre information. On the other hand, some of the larger respected sites contain valuable information in a well-organized format that can save you time and effort when you're looking for something specific.

Some Valuable Coaches' Sites to Check Out:

Basketball Highway
The Basketball coaches' homepage.
http://www.bbhighway.com

C.O.A.C.H
An online service for Football Coaches
http://www.coachhelp.com

Coaches' Edge
A one-stop technology solution site.
http://www.coachesedge.com

USA Coaches' Clinics
Clinic, books, video and software information for coaches.
http://www.usacoaches.com

Cybertown's Coaches Corner
Speak directly with coaches from all sports around the world.
http://www.cybertown.net/wi/syskos

Part
4

The Media: Friend or Foe?

Coaching Youth Sports
An electronic newsletter for coaches, athletes, and parents; provided by Virginia Tech University. Purpose: to present information about learning and performing sport skills.
http://www.chre.vt.edu/~/cys/

The Best Source is You!

Fans and colleagues, who want accurate information about your team and organization, want to hear it straight from the source. This means that if you don't already have an official website or access to one through your organization, you should get one. This site can be a forum for you, to promote your team's victories and to deal with the losses. Keep the following things in mind when considering your website:

1 Be Realistic... and Delegate
Before you start to think "Great, another thing for me to worry about," relax. You're a busy person, and probably don't have the time to monitor a website. The solution is to delegate the project to a professional within or outside of your organization. Then, you don't have to worry about the mechanics involved. Keep an eye on the content of your website, and leave others to worry about the rest.

2 Remember, Communication is a Two-Way Street
Once you have a website that people use and recognize, you have an invaluable tool at your fingertips. Keep close contact with the person in charge of maintaining the site, and offer suggestions and pointers. Double check to make sure that there are no mistakes. Web sites today have all kinds of interactive features, such as chat rooms, surveys, and web-based training. These are all features that can be used on your official website. For instance, if you're having doubts about your team's image, your site could include a survey that asks readers about their perception of your team. You could also invite fans to chat about a recent event, or to discuss a particular relevant issue.

All of these suggestions will help you to drum up interest among your fans and colleagues using your website. It will also give you valuable feedback about the public's perception of your team. It's a terrific marketing tool when done well!

Things to Keep in Mind About the Internet

The Internet is a great resource for you, your team, and your organization, but like any public medium, it has its positives and negatives. This isn't a reason to dismiss it, just view anything you see on the Internet with skepticism, and remember the following points.

1 It has a widespread reach.

2 Information moves incredibly fast.

3 There are a variety of forums - including chat groups, news groups, and bulletin boards - both paid and free.

4 It contains both fact and fiction.

5 There are no standards of accuracy.

Part

4

Foe?

PLAY BY PLAY

What the Internet Can Do For You

1 Minimize Risks
To minimize the risk of misinformation, you can have a media press kit and media response page on your official website with immediately available, accurate information.

2 Monitor Rumors
Not everyone knows the difference between a legitimate site and an illegitimate one, so you need a highly visible and respected website to set the record straight when rumors are flying.

3 Maximize Exposure
You can attract positive attention with your site, from fans and from the media. To keep in touch with fans, schedule live chats between fans and athletes or coaches, and allow fans to send email to the team.

WORKSHEET

Media Quiz:
Are You an Effective Spokesperson?

When you're asked to do an interview either during practice, after a big event, or just on a normal day, are you sending the right messages?

When giving an interview, do you look the interviewer in the eyes?   Yes   No

When answering questions, do you use cliches and fillers?   Yes   No

Before giving an interview, are you aware of whom will be receiving your message?   Yes   No

During an interview, are you genuine and enthusiastic?   Yes   No

When you answer questions, do you use jargon and ambiguous terms?   Yes   No

(Desired answers: Yes, No, Yes, Yes, No.)

Your answers to the previous questions will help you to figure out the quality of your interview etiquette. Being an effective spokesperson allows you to express your ideas clearly while enhancing your image. Refer to the checklists on the following page to understand *why* your answers should match those above.

WORKSHEET

Media Quiz: Are You an Effective Spokesperson? con't

An Effective Spokesperson . . .

❏ *Paints Pictures With Words*

❏ *Is Genuine*

❏ *Avoids Cliches and Fillers*

❏ *Seems Enthusiastic*

❏ *Knows the Audience*

❏ *Gives Good Quotes*

An Ineffective Spokesperson . . .

❏ *Talks Too Fast / Slow*

❏ *Can't Stand Still*

❏ *Uses Cliches / Fillers*

❏ *Doesn't Help the Public Understand*

❏ *Seems Bored and Boring*

❏ *Looks Down / Away*

WORKSHEET

Media Quiz:
Are You an Effective Spokesperson? con't

Interview Prep Checklist

Use this checklist before every interview to ensure that you're prepared. If you have additional notes, or comments that you want to remember, add them at the end.

Interviewer:

_____

_____

Date of Interview:

_____

Interview Topic / Angle:

_____

_____

Interviewer / News Outlet:

_____

_____

Previous position taken on topic:

_____

_____

Interview style:

_____

_____

WORKSHEET

Media Quiz:
Are You an Effective Spokesperson? con't

Ultimate audience I'm speaking to:

_____

_____

_____

Others being interviewed:
(Anticipate their angle and its effect on your content.)

_____

_____

_____

My primary theme for this interview:
(One complete, concise sentence that conveys your focus.)

_____

_____

_____

Notes / Comments:

_____

_____

_____

_____

_____

_____

_____

_____

_____

_____

_____

Part 5

Crisis Communication

When you make a mistake,
there are only three things
you should ever do about it:
[1] admit it, [2] learn from it,
and [3] don't repeat it.

Bear Bryant
Former football coach,
University of Alabama

CHAPTER 24
When It Hits the Fan!

"Prep Athlete Suffers Dangerous Head Injury."

"Olympic Runner Tested for Steroids."

"NCAA Troubled by Bad Behavior, Coaching Woes."

"Stadium Balcony Collapse Kills 22."

You've read the headlines *about teams in trouble. One day those headlines could be about your team. Media scrutiny of teams and their athletes shows no signs of going away. When something negative happens, the first person people look to is the coach - so whether the crisis turns into an opportunity or a disaster depends on* **your response.**

Avoiding a Potential Crisis

Be Specific

Avoid lumping minor incidents in with the most heinous. If you say that an athlete broke team rules, people assume the worst, like he was arrested, when it may mean he was late to one practice.

Know the Difference Between a Problem and a Crisis

Blowing a small incident out of proportion may create a crisis where there was none before, while underestimating another incident may result in needless negative publicity and wasted efforts. Divide your potential problems into one of three categories: *incident, emergency, or crisis.* Only then can you identify what must be done. There are three things you must do when formulating a crisis plan: *predict, prepare, and practice.*

Have A Crisis Plan

A crisis can be an athlete arrested, an athlete with academic deficiencies, personnel issues, or anything that's out of your control. A well-developed *Crisis Management Plan* will help you deal with these chaotic situations. This doesn't have to be your job alone - you should form a "crisis team." This can include: your Athletic Director, your Sports Information or Media Relations Director, the college president, the owner, a PR professional, an outside consultant, or your staff. All of these people are resources who can help you before, during, and after a crisis.

A Crisis Management Plan will:

1 Speed response time.

2 Heighten confidence.

3 Limit liability.

The first step is to decide which problems can develop into high impact crises, and which ones are low. Then, identify your resources and use them to your advantage. Another valuable resource is your counterpart at another institution, who may have dealt with a similar problem before.

The coach, AD, and when necessary the university president, owner, or other official should work out how to handle a crisis before it happens. If you don't, there will be a great deal of confusion and a degree of paralysis when something does go wrong.

The severity of the issue determines the level of organizational involvement. In some cases, the university or organization has to lead the crisis response. This will take pressure off of you, but if changes are made to policy and procedure, you have to live with them.

CHAPTER 25
Vigilant Thinking

Crisis preparation begins with prevention and anticipation. Be a "vigilant thinker." Watch other programs, on any level, and look for trends. Look at general population trends, too. For instance: If activism and youth rebellion are on the rise, what does this mean for your program?

This planning process usually leads to endless streams of questions that can produce extreme distress and restless nights. So why do it? The issue is one of control. Do you want to control your team's future? Or would you prefer letting circumstances beat you and your team, and dictate your destiny?

By anticipating a response when a crisis hits, you'll be better prepared. No matter how much you'd like the controversy to disappear, **timeliness** and **an appropriate response** are critical. With a crisis management document, procedures will be clear and you'll have critical names and phone numbers immediately available, even on weekends, holidays, and when you're on the road.

POINTERS➔

Planning Your Crisis Management Plan

In order to begin the Crisis Management Planning Process, four initial questions must be asked:

1 *What types of crises are your team susceptible to?*

2 *What is the potential impact of each?*

3 *What is the probability of a specific crisis occurring, based on the history of your program, current personnel and resources, organizational structure, environment, social mores, etc.?*

4 *What is your current level of preparedness?*

Consider the Impact of a Crisis

You have to deal with both the short and long-term ramifications of a crisis. In the short term, a crisis can harm the image and credibility of you and your team, and in some cases, your institution. You'll get intense negative scrutiny from the public and the media. You need to address those outside audiences but you cannot forget your internal audiences. The athletes, staff, administration, faculty and alumni are some of those inside your organization that need to be addressed. If you communicate well with those inside, they can be your best ambassadors of good will and help the healing process.

Long term, you may be facing no post-season play, or loss of television exposure that costs your institution or organization money and reputation. *What about your job?* All are things to think about now, when you're not dealing with a crisis.

Risk Management

Crises will always go away. How you handle them determines the legacy they will leave behind. "Preparation is always better when done in advance." In other words, you must plan ahead to avoid and/or manage potential crises. Frankly, most institutions are poorly prepared to professionally handle a crisis in a fast, efficient and confident manner. Coach involvement is often vital to the effective communication of crisis management issues, decisions, and ramifications. Keep the following points in mind regarding risk management and prevention.

To Effectively Communicate Risk Management Policies, Procedures and Sensitivities...

1 Understand the scope of legal responsibilities that comes with assuming a coaching position, i.e. proper supervision, planning and instruction, matching participants, safety, first aid and risk management.

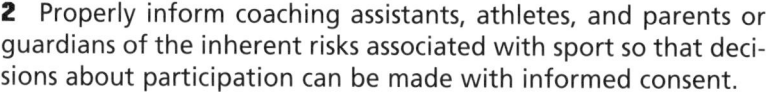

2 Properly inform coaching assistants, athletes, and parents or guardians of the inherent risks associated with sport so that decisions about participation can be made with informed consent.

3 Know and convey the need and availability of appropriate medical insurance.

4 Participate in continuing education regarding rules changes, improvements in equipment, philosophical changes, improved techniques and other information in order to enhance the safety and success of the athlete.

These are national standards for athletic coaches, set by the National Association for Sport and Physical Education. Additional coaching standards and related information can be found at their website: http://www.aahperd.org/naspe/naspe.html

Liability

Having a crisis plan in place can save a coaching career and prevent massive financial loss by everyone concerned. Unfortunately, in many instances, a coach puts too much time and effort into his game plan and not enough into having a plan when it comes to liability and negligence.

The **American Football Coaches Association,** for example, reminds its coaches through its publications that "failure to warn" is usually one of the primary accusations made against coaches in litigation involving catastrophic injury to an athlete. The AFCA makes the following suggestions to help coaches avoid such liability:

1 Have a clear and complete understanding of the intent and correct application of safety rules.

2 Make graphically clear to athletes the risk of violating these rules and use printed material to remind them of correct techniques.

3 Point out in exact terms the risk of accidental catastrophic injury in athletics before the first practice begins.

(Provided by the *American Football Coaches Association*)

A coach who has little awareness of the risks involved in his profession, and how to address them, is in dire need of issues management training and a comprehensive crisis plan.

Be Cautious when Handling Possible Criminal Activities

Watch out for Confessions.

Because athletes trust you, you become a confidant and in cases of criminal activity this can get you a subpoena. There are no laws that protect athlete/coach relationships. You're better off referring your athlete to a lawyer.

Avoid Accepting Potential Evidence.

A NCAA coach thought he was helping an athlete who asked him to hold a weapon. The coach was subsequently severely chastised for holding potential criminal evidence. Intentions don't matter here. The law does. If you try to protect athletes in these circumstances, you hurt all parties involved and put yourself at risk.

The Best Way to Prepare!

Developing a comprehensive and usable crisis plan is complex and time consuming, but highly valuable. The best way to accomplish this goal is with professional help from companies like *Sports Media Challenge* and others that have significant real life experience in this area. It is also important that those experts understand the uniqueness of sports and the needs of your organization. Once a crisis document is developed, crisis management training will take your readiness to the next level, and is highly recommended.

For more information, see Contact Information p. 163 or *visit us on the web at:* www.sports.mediachallenge.com

CHAPTER 26
Crisis and the Media

When a crisis hits, you will hear from the media. Remember that they aren't the crisis, but they certainly will magnify it. It's important to prepare yourself, the athletes, and all other representatives for media questions. The following pointers will help you keep control of the situation.

PLAY BY PLAY

Dealing with the Media in Hot Situations

All interview requests should be filtered appropriately through the institution's higher authorities: the AD, the SID, Media Relations, the Public Information Office, or the Public Relations Department.

Track and log rumors, you'll find them in the media reports, on the Internet, by logging questions received over the phone, and by checking with your own personnel.

Analyze them to help anticipate what may happen next and the intensity of public reaction.

Log requests for information, such as who's asking for what, and the response.

Monitor all media stories to anticipate the intensity and direction of public/media reaction.

Call in corrections to any significant misinformation immediately.

Anticipate the next angle the media will take.

Using the Net to Set the Record Straight

One source of rumor and misinformation, which we have mentioned before, is the Internet. It's part of crisis management to monitor the Internet so that you can be aware of what people are being exposed to. You can also use the Internet to your advantage, responding to misinformation and posting corrections where the fans will see it. This should not be your personal responsibility, but it will be valuable for you to periodically take a look.

CHAPTER 27
Trauma Counseling

A student-athlete dies of kidney and heart failure after a 2-hour workout in a hot sauna. Random violence takes the life of a star football player destined for the NFL. A professional athlete is diagnosed with a potentially terminal disease at the start of the season.

Traumatic events such as these can happen every day, and they have a devastating effect on the people directly and indirectly involved. Athletic teams draw their character and much of their success from closeness, interdependency and chemistry among their members - so when a team faces a crisis, everyone involved is affected.

What does this mean for a coach? If you're faced with an event for which you're unprepared, document the steps you take while handling it, so that you can consult them when planning for the next crisis.

First and foremost, make sure your athletic department has a comprehensive *Crisis Management Plan.* It should at the very least lay out priority steps, phone numbers, and outside experts needed to respond to the crisis and the ensuing need for internal and external communication. The media is a critical component here. A speedy, *caring* response is essential for real and perceived reasons.

Avoid "Business as Usual"

How can a coach deal with such a situation? By using an often-neglected crisis management tool: Post-Trauma Counseling. Experts contend that it's inappropriate to act as if nothing happened and assume business as usual.

Athletes and staff look to their coach for direction, so how does one deal with the aftermath of a traumatic experience? Emotions are very high after a trauma, so you must refocus your team for the season. Often, coaches find that trauma can be a

STEP BY STEP

Keys to Coping

1 Assess the Team's Needs
Because degrees of trauma vary, you must first assess their needs both as a group and as individuals.
Ask yourself: *Are school counselors and ministers needed, or should I bring in professional post-trauma counselors and sports psychologists?*

2 Act Fast
Crisis planning within the first 24 hours is critical.
For example, what if the crisis happens on the road?
When a traumatic experience occurs while your team's away, the confusion and lag time are multiplied.
You'll need extra help because you don't have the same resources available that you do at home.

3 Consult Your Peers
Another key to dealing with traumatic events is to look to assistants, trainers and other coaches to see if they've dealt with similar situations. Most will be more than happy to share the lessons they've learned.

4 Care About Your Team Members and Staff
The well being of your team and staff is your primary concern. If it's not your style to be warm and talkative, attentive listening can effectively convey your compassion in most circumstances.

tremendous motivational tool; using symbols such as black armbands, a seat reserved on the bench, a preserved locker, or jersey/number retirement.

Post-Trauma Counseling Can Help

It's not unusual for coaches or athletes to avoid post-trauma counseling. There's something inherent about sports that convinces participants that they don't need help coping. How do you deal with this?

Make the first meeting with a counselor mandatory. Let them gripe about it, but **make them go** so that the counselor can assess whether or not further counseling is necessary for some or all of those involved.

On the most basic level, this initial counseling is most helpful because it lets recipients know what is and isn't a normal reaction. This means that the counselor can find out, for example, whether a teammate is having nightmares or feeling depressed, and for how long a period. They can then decide whether he or she is experiencing a normal reaction, or if there's a more serious problem.

Post-trauma counseling benefits you and your team in the long run. Counseling helps people sort out emotions and gain closure while reinforcing the solidarity of the group.

WORKSHEET

Crisis Worksheet

Remember that the first step toward creating a Crisis Management Plan is to predict. Start by identifying your potential crises, based on the examples given in this chapter.

Potential Crises:

_____

_____

_____

_____

_____

The next step is to assess the *impact* of your potential crises. Do this by placing them in one of the following categories:

1 Incident
Examples: Rumors of sexual harassment, drop in ticket sales, threat of academic ineligibility.

_____

_____

_____

_____

_____

2 Emergency
Examples: High profile contract disputes, threat of lawsuit, prominent, sustained negative coverage.

_____

_____

_____

_____

WORKSHEET

Crisis Worksheet con't

3 Crisis
Examples: NCAA major violation, high profile athlete convicted of felony, stampede in stadium causing injuries.

_____

_____

_____

_____

_____

The higher the impact of the crisis, the more senior administrators should be immediately involved and the more resources you will need. Make a list of your available resources, based on the examples given in this chapter and by evaluating case studies or through professional guidance.

Resources:

_____

_____

_____

_____

_____

_____

_____

_____

_____

_____

_____

_____

_____

Wrapping It Up

Without organization and
leadership toward a
realistic goal, there is
no chance of realizing more
than a small percentage
of your potential.

John Wooden
Former Head Coach At UCLA
NCAA Record Setter

Conclusion

The team breathes a sigh of relief as their coach dismisses practice early one afternoon. She gives a brief talk to the athletes and sends them on their way, watching them head off to the locker room. The coach returns to her office, where she changes into a suit.

She heads toward a meeting in which key administrators are meeting to discuss the reallocation of funds within the athletic program. She makes a brief presentation to the assembled group, then asks for questions. When asked for specifics on what she'd do with additional funding, she details clear-cut needs and even suggests some luxuries that her rivals count as fundamental and use as recruiting draws. She delivers the information calmly and confidently, then sits down.

Later, the coach finds out that the administrators have increased her budget and she can breathe easily for one more year.

As we explained in the Introduction to this book - your career, your reputation, even your livelihood can depend on how you communicate as a coach. If it were up to you, you might opt to be a coach in the strictest sense - leading practice and events only - but your job is no longer that simple. It probably never was!

This is Your Playbook - Use It!

The **Coach's Communication Playbook** was not written to tell you how to coach, it was written to give you the tools you need to be a better communicator - and better communicators are better coaches.

Some of the communication tips found in this book are the same that are given to corporate executives, professional speakers, politicians, doctors, lawyers, and other members of the corporate world - with one very important difference. They're tailored to help coaches like you to better deal with the complexity, versatility, and spontaneity of your profession as it has evolved. This book will supplement your coaching skills, allowing you to focus on what's important to you while communicating effectively to those around you.

This isn't a book to be read - it's a book to be *used*. So as you use it, mold it to suit your needs. Highlight sections that you find more useful, and dog-ear the pages. Use the worksheets over and over, charting your progress. If you continue to use the *Playbook* as a reference, you will start to incorporate the ideas inside as part of your everyday communication.

Talk Back to Us!

Communication is a two-way street. So far in this book, however, we've been talking to you. Now it's your turn! Tell us the real life stories that have happened to you or other coaches and athletes, bloopers and all!

Share Your Stories

We'd also like to know about real life situations where you've applied the strategies and techniques within this book - and what the results were. How did you adapt a tip to make it work better for you, a specific athlete, or a team?

Do you have your own proven tips or suggestions that you'd like to share with your coaching peers across the country?

We may include your stories and suggestions in future editions of *The Coach's Communication Playbook.* And, of course, we'll give credit where credit's due.

CONTACT INFORMATION

Sports Media Challenge

Address:	Attn.: Talk Back
	Sports Media Challenge
	2700 Coltsgate Road, Suite 203
	Charlotte, NC 28211
Phone:	(704) 365-5027
Fax:	(704) 366-9556
Email:	info@sports.mediachallenge.com
Website:	www.sports.mediachallenge.com

To order *SMC* products, call: 1-800-929-4386

Appendix

References

1 Robertson, Jeanne. *Don't Let the Funny Stuff Get Away: Turn Everyday Experiences into Stories Audiences Will Remember.* Houston, TX: Rich Publishing Company, 1998.

2 Dubrin, Andrew J. *Personal Magnetism: Discover Your Own Charisma and Learn to Charm, Inspire, and Influence Others.* New York: AMACOM, 1997.

Additional Resources

We just couldn't resist giving you more useful information. The following is a guide to additional resources, some of which are mentioned in this book, which can help you be an outstanding communicator.

Resources by Subject:

Communication
How to Be a Great Communicator :
In Person, on Paper, and on the Podium.
> Qubein, Nido R. New York: John Wiley & Sons, Incorporated, 1996.
> ISBN 0-4711-6314-7. Retail Price: $16.95.
> Available in bookstores.

Humor
Don't Let the Funny Stuff Get Away: Turn Everyday Experiences into Stories Audiences Will Remember.
> Robertson, Jeanne. Houston, TX:
> Rich Publishing Company, 1998.
> ISBN 0-9275-7703-8. Price: $15.00.
> To order, call: (336) 584-9641 or email: jeannetalk@aol.com.

Storytelling
Story Selling ™ is a concept designed by Dr. Paul Homoly.
> Products and workshops are available from the *Homoly Marketing Group*. To order, call: (704) 342-4900 or email: phomoly@mindspring.com.

Coaching Magnetism
Personal Magnetism: Discover Your Own Charisma and Learn to Charm, Inspire, and Influence Others.
> Dubrin, Andrew J. New York: AMACOM, 1997.
> ISBN 0-8144-7936-7. Retail Price: $16.95.
> Available in bookstores.

Networking
How to Work a Room: Learn the Strategies of Savvy Socializing for Business and Personal Success
RoAne, Susan. New York: Warner Books, 1989.
Retail Price: $11.99. Available in bookstores.

Image
Character Is Everything: Promoting Ethical Excellence in Sports.
Gough, Russell W. New York: Harcourt Brace College Publishers, 1998.
ISBN 0-1550-3528-2. Retail Price: $18.50.
Available in bookstores.

Attitude and Motivation
Permission to Win.
Pelletier, Ray. Oak Hill Press, 1996.
ISBN 1-8869-3910-1. Retail Price: $22.95.
Available in bookstores.

The Media
The Pocket Guide to Avoiding Misquotes.
Hessert, Kathleen. Charlotte, NC: Sports Media Challenge, 1991.
Retail Price: $2.50. Available from SMC.
To order, call: 1-800-929-4386 or email: info@sports.mediachallenge.com.

Power Training: How to Win at the Media Game, an Audio Series.
Hessert, Kathleen. Charlotte, NC: Sports Media Challenge, 1996.
Retail Price: $49.95. Available from SMC.
To order, call: 1-800-929-4386 or email: info@sports.mediachallenge.com.

Mastering the News Media Interview : How to Succeed at Television, Radio, and Print Interviews.
Rafe, Stephen C.
Starfire/Rapport Communications, 1991.
Retail Price: $24.95. Available in bookstores.

PRODUCT ORDER FORM

Call 1-800-929-4386 or 704-365-3756
or e-mail: info@sports.mediachallenge.com

The Coach's Communication Playbook
Developing Communication Champions **$15.95**

Power Training:
How to Win at the Media Game
Audio Series **$49.95**

The Pocket Guide to Avoiding Misquotes
Pocket Reference Guide **$2.50**

The ABC's to Responding to Challenging Comments
Pocket Reference Card **$2.50**

The 1998 Hessert Sports Crisis Survey
A Full Report, Including Complete Results,
Analysis, and Comparison with
1994 Survey Results **$69.95**

I'm a Kid... Run With Me
Training Log and Diary for Young People **$12.95**

Shipping and Handling additional.

Bulk rates available.

For more information contact Sports Media Challenge at
1-800-929-4386 or 704-365-3756 *(within North Carolina)*
or visit our website: www.sports.mediachallenge.com

control of, 35; ABC's of, 35; reinforcing message through, 34; tough questions during, 127-131

Recruiting, 81-84; answering questions, 181, 183; talking to families, 81-84; tips for, 83-84

References, 165

Rehearsal, 64

Representing Your Team, 97-98; to the media, 99, 101; to the outside world, 98, 101; to your AD, 73-76; *(see also Image)*

Resources, 167-168

Respect, 35, 53, 82, 84, 105, 106

Risk Management, 148; and student confidentiality, 116; and off the record comments, 127; *(see also Liability)*

Share Your Stories, 162

Soundbites, 25, 114, 133

Speaking Skills, and interpersonal communications, 68-89; presentation and delivery, 24-61; worksheet, content, 90-91; worksheet, preparation, 62-65

Speaking Worksheet, Content, 90-91; Preparation, 62-65

Spokesperson, 139-40; choosing the right, during a crisis, 146, effective, 139-40; ineffective, 140; checklist, 139-140

Sports Information Departments/ Directors, and crisis, 151; and the media, 77-80; and media resources, 78-80; and media training, 79-80; sending introduction, 48

Stage Presence, 41 *(see also Delivery)*

Storytelling, 58-60; as motivational tool, 38; using humorous stories, 53-55; in presentations, 58-60; story selling by Dr. Paul Homoly, 58, 167; to create an impact, 59

Student Confidentiality, 116 *(see also Buckley Amendment)*

Sympathy, 62

Talk Back, 162

Trust, 19, 22, 27, 69, 70, 82-84

Values, 37, 49, 96, 98

Videotape, providing for the media, 126; as a preparation tool, 80; as a visual aid, when being interviewed, 114, 118-120

Vigilant Thinking, 147-150

Visibility, 99; all eyes on you, 101; keeping in perspective, 101-103; *(see also Image)*

Visuals, 39; checking your equipment, 64; motivational visuals, 39; using, 39, 69; visual impact, 39